architecture
materials
wood bois holz

architecture
materials
wood bois holz

evergreen

© 2008 EVERGREEN GmbH, Köln

Editorial coordination, editor: Simone Schleifer
Text: Florian Seidel
English translation: Amy Brooke for LocTeam, Barcelona
French translation: Claire Débard for LocTeam, Barcelona
German proof-reading: Michael Heinrich for LocTeam,
Barcelona
Typesetting and text editing: LocTeam, Barcelona
Art director: Mireia Casanovas Soley
Graphic design and layout: Laura Millán

ISBN 978-3-8365-0403-4

Printed in China

Contents
Sommaire
Inhalt

Introduction

Wood is the oldest and most alive building material available. It has many advantages: it can be found almost everywhere in the world, it can be used for many purposes and it is easy to work with.

The tree is one of the most important, most comprehensive and most significant symbols for man. The origin of wood and its thousand-year-old involvement as a building material in our cultural history have given rise to our intense emotional bonds with it. We feel close to this warm, organic material, closer than to cold stone or to transitory clay. It is no coincidence that the first toys young children have are often made from wood. Wood surrounds us in our daily lives, in much the same way as clothes do, and makes our surroundings homely.

Even these days, wood can still compete with any high-tech material. Wood has an extremely favourable strength-to-weight ratio and outstanding acoustic qualities. It appears in countless different forms, from wood chip to fibreboard. In regions at a high risk of earthquakes, for example, wood has been used as a building material for thousands of years because it can absorb tremors. More recently, wood is back in favour thanks to its environmentally-friendly and energy-saving characteristics. Since time immemorial, buildings made from wood have complied with the low-energy standards so important today. Erecting and demolishing a wooden structure is climate-neutral and environmentally friendly, as no more carbon dioxide is released than was absorbed by photosynthesis when the tree was growing.

As a natural product, wood is certainly not a homogeneous building material. The characteristics of the longitudinal and horizontal fibres can differ greatly from one type of wood to another. This is equally true for its water absorption, structural stability, acoustic and thermal properties and appearance. Even within a particular type or cross-section of wood, the way it develops means that there are vast differences which must be carefully observed when using it. Wood shrinks, it "works", it can catch fire at relatively low temperatures. The weaknesses of wood are also an intrinsic part of its nature.

Advances in building technology have also led to the further development of wood as a building material. Glue, paint and coatings are specifically used to counter wood's natural weaknesses, and it is almost impossible to imagine using wood as we do today without them. Frequently, natural wood is no longer used, instead we see multi-layered glued boards, synthetic carrier materials with a wood surface or engineered wood boards made from very different compositions. The capacity for innovation in the field of wood technology seems to know no bounds. However, the precision and invisible joints which are often requested today can hardly ever be achieved with wood. The dimensions of any form of timber are more limited than those of other building materials. Wood constructions must still be "joined" from individual elements. Therefore, the architect must, as a basic principle, be very precise and deliberate in his designs. However, he can frequently make use of old, traditional techniques and experience.

Today, wood is often used as a test material and laboratory for young, unknown architects, as it costs relatively little and is also comparatively cheap to work. Lower building costs increase the scope for experimentation and creative voyages of discovery. This is literally true: wooden constructions are usually produced in the workshop; they can then be relatively easily transported in sections even to remote locations, where they can be quickly assembled.

Wood is in the process of losing its image as a cheap building material because it offers the advantages of durability and stability in comparison with synthetic building materials. Wood forgives no construction errors and no decisions that go against logic and simplicity. Ill-considered detailing that adheres to current trends but neglects to protect the wood means that in no time, upon exposure to the elements, the wood turns unsightly. Long-term, penetrating humidity leads to rotting and infestation. We can see what today's architects are really capable of in their work with wood. Those who know and use wood's natural qualities have a wonderfully versatile material at their disposal which can come to life in the hands of a creative designer and builder.

The capacity to transform and adapt – which makes wood a "human" building material – is visible and its most exclusive quality. Wood reflects every type of lighting, every type of weather and every season. Wood ages, shows character and lets us read history from it (assuming a certain amount of protective care).

Wood is particularly expressive when used in conjunction with other materials. Depending on its application, it can have a raw and rough-and-ready effect, or it can caress the hand as a precisely-finished piece of furniture, it can radiate severity or play on its tactile qualities. A raw surface, broken up in many places, can contrast with its warmth and sleekness, while a smooth, jointless surface can appear refined in juxtaposition to its lively, organic structure. It can produce a variety of effects, regardless of its environment: delicate, transitory and light, or solid, robust and weighty. Surfaces which are left natural, glazed in bright colours or painted wooden surfaces each boost the effect of the other. For buildings in natural landscapes, wood comes naturally to mind as a building material because it nestles so harmoniously into its surroundings. The deliberate two-dimensional use of industrially-produced derived timber products, such as chipboards, creates attractive effects set against an urban background and leads to applications that were previously not possible.

Today, wood is seen as a design challenge, and again and again projects question the correct shape, the simple solution and the logical answer. They continue to do this in their own way and in their own context, which is why the projects all look so different at first glance. But they all have one thing in common: the visible use of wood always forges a relationship between the building and the person using or looking at it.

Introduction

Le bois est le matériau de construction le plus vivant dont dispose l'humanité, sans doute aussi le plus ancien. Ses avantages : on le trouve presque partout dans le monde, il a des usages multiples et il est facile à travailler.

Pour l'homme, l'arbre compte parmi les symboles les plus importants, les plus absolus et les plus profonds qui soient. Le fait que le bois vienne de l'arbre et le rôle qu'il joue dans l'histoire de la civilisation humaine depuis des millénaires a tissé des liens affectifs étroits entre l'homme et le bois. Nous le percevons comme chaud et vivant et nous nous sentons proches de lui, plus proches que de la pierre froide ou de l'argile éphémère. Ce n'est pas un hasard si les premiers jouets des enfants sont souvent en bois. De plus en plus l'homme s'entoure de bois dans sa vie quotidienne et c'est le bois qui rend son environnement agréable à vivre.

Ses qualités permettent au bois, encore aujourd'hui, de rivaliser avec les matériaux les plus modernes. Il présente un rapport résistance/poids exceptionnel et ses propriétés acoustiques sont excellentes. On le trouve sous les formes les plus diverses, du bardeau au panneau de fibres agglomérées. Dans les régions exposées aux tremblements de terre, on utilise le bois pour les constructions depuis des millénaires car il absorbe les secousses sismiques. Ses propriétés climatiques et énergétiques l'ont également remis à l'honneur depuis peu. En effet, les bâtiments en bois répondent depuis toujours aux normes actuelles en matière de basse consommation d'énergie ; leur construction n'a aucune répercussion sur le climat et ils peuvent être recyclés écologiquement après leur démolition car la photosynthèse des plantes fixe le dioxyde de carbone de l'atmosphère dans le bois.

Mais parce qu'il est issu de la croissance des plantes, le bois n'est pas un matériau homogène. Il présente parfois des caractéristiques très différentes selon le sens de la coupe, parallèle ou perpendiculaire aux fibres – absorption de l'eau, stabilité statique, propriétés acoustiques et thermiques ou aspect. On peut aussi rencontrer ce genre de disparités dans une même essence, voire dans une même coupe transversale, particularités qu'il faut prendre en compte lors de l'utilisation du bois. Par ailleurs, le bois se contracte, il « travaille » et il peut s'enflammer à une température relativement basse. Mais ses faiblesses sont elles aussi indissociables de son caractère.

Le bois doit aussi son développement aux progrès de la construction. L'emploi de colles, peintures et revêtements compense ses faiblesses naturelles et fait aujourd'hui partie intégrante de son exploitation. Souvent, on n'utilise plus du bois massif, mais plusieurs couches de panneaux collés, des matériaux supports synthétiques recouverts d'une surface de bois ou des matériaux dérivés du bois aux compositions les plus diverses. La capacité d'innovation des hommes semble illimitée en ce qui concerne le bois.

Pourtant, le bois ne permettra jamais d'obtenir les surfaces planes et sans jointures souvent recherchées de nos jours et les dimensions du bois d'œuvre, quelle que soit sa forme, sont toujours plus limitées que celles d'autres matériaux. Encore aujourd'hui, les constructions en bois doivent être assemblées à partir d'éléments individuels, ce qui exige des architectes des réalisations extrêmement précises et des détails parfaitement réfléchis. Souvent cependant, ils peuvent tirer profit des méthodes traditionnelles et des expériences du passé.

Aujourd'hui, le bois tient souvent lieu de mise à l'épreuve et de test pour les jeunes architectes encore peu connus en raison de son prix d'achat relativement bas et de son usinage comparativement moins onéreux que celui d'autres matériaux. Les coûts de construction réduits laissent une plus grande marge de manœuvre pour faire toutes sortes d'expériences et recherches créatives. Au sens propre du terme d'ailleurs, car les constructions en bois sont pour la plupart réalisées en atelier, d'où elles peuvent facilement être transportées en pièces détachées jusqu'aux endroits les plus reculés pour y être remontées en peu de temps.

Au vu de ses incontestables atouts, le bois est néanmoins sur le point de perdre son image de matériau bon marché car, par rapport à de nombreux matériaux de construction synthétiques, il présente l'avantage de la résistance et de la stabilité. En revanche, le bois ne pardonne aucune erreur de construction, ni aucun choix contraire aux lois de la logique et de la simplicité. Des détails insuffisamment pensés, comme c'est souvent le cas aujourd'hui pour des raisons de mode, qui ne tiennent pas compte de la nécessaire protection du matériau, lui font rapidement perdre tout son éclat dès qu'il est exposé aux intempéries car la pénétration permanente d'humidité entraîne le pourrissement et des attaques de nuisibles. C'est à leur rapport avec le bois qu'on reconnaît ce que les architectes actuels sont vraiment capables de réaliser.

En revanche, connaître et tirer profit des qualités naturelles du bois, c'est disposer d'un matériau merveilleusement polyvalent qui s'éveille à la vie sous les mains créatrices des concepteurs et des artisans.

Les capacités d'adaptation et de transformation qui font du bois un matériau de construction « humain » sont aussi son expression la plus visible et sa qualité la plus distinguée. Le bois reflète les changements de lumière, le temps, les saisons ; il vieillit, ne manque pas de caractère et laisse l'histoire se lire en lui pour peu qu'il ait bénéficié des soins nécessaires à sa préservation.

Le bois déploie tout particulièrement sa personnalité lorsqu'il est associé à d'autres matériaux. Selon l'emploi qui en est fait, il peut paraître grossier et raboteux ou flatter la main sous la forme d'un meuble raffiné et parfaitement fini, il peut respirer la force ou montrer ses qualités tactiles. Sa chaleur et sa douceur peuvent contraster avec une surface rêche aux multiples brisures, sa structure organique et vivante peut affiner une surface lisse sans jointures. Selon ce qui l'entoure, il peut paraître gracieux, fragile et léger ou massif, robuste et lourd. Les surfaces laissées au naturel et le bois lasuré ou peint de couleurs vives se mettent mutuellement en valeur. Dans les paysages naturels, le bois est le matériau de construction qui s'impose de lui-même tant il se coule harmonieusement dans l'environnement. Dans un cadre urbain, l'utilisation de matériaux obtenus par procédé industriel en fonction des besoins, par exemple différents panneaux de particules, produit de ravissants effets et ouvre des perspectives d'emplois du bois jusqu'alors impossibles.

Les projets qui s'emparent aujourd'hui du bois comme d'un défi créatif posent sans cesse la question de la forme la plus adéquate, de la solution la plus simple, de la réponse la plus logique. Ils la résolvent chacun à leur manière et dans leur contexte propre, ce qui explique qu'ils paraissent tous si différents à première vue. Pourtant, ils ont tous quelque chose en commun : le bois apparent place toujours l'édifice dans un certain rapport avec l'homme qui l'utilise ou l'observe.

Einleitung

Holz ist der lebendigste und zugleich wohl älteste Baustoff, über den die Menschheit verfügt. Seine Vorteile: Er kommt fast überall auf der Welt vor, ist vielseitig verwendbar und leicht zu bearbeiten.

Eines der wichtigsten, umfassendsten und tiefsten Symbole des Menschen ist der Baum. Die Herkunft des Holzes aus dem Baum und die jahrtausende alte Verflechtung des Baustoffs Holz mit der Kulturgeschichte der Menschheit hat eine enge emotionale Verbindung des Menschen zum Holz entstehen lassen. Wir fühlen uns dem als warm und organisch empfundenen Material Holz nahe, näher als dem kalten Stein oder dem vergänglichen Lehm. Nicht von ungefähr ist das erste Spielzeug des Kleinkinds häufig aus Holz gefertigt. Holz umgibt den Menschen in seinem täglichen Leben und macht sein Umfeld erst wohnlich.

Aufgrund seiner stofflichen Eigenschaften macht Holz auch in unserer Zeit jedem High-Tech-Werkstoff Konkurrenz. Holz besitzt ein außerordentlich günstiges Verhältnis von Festigkeit zu Gewicht, und es hat hervorragende akustische Eigenschaften. Es tritt in zahllosen unterschiedlichen Formen auf, von der Holzschindel bis zur Faserplatte. Seit Jahrtausenden wird zum Beispiel in erdbebengefährdeten Regionen mit Holz gebaut, das die Erdstöße aufnehmen kann, und in jüngster Zeit ist Holz auch durch seine das Klima schonenden und energiesparenden Eigenschaften wieder zu Ehren gelangt. Aus Holz errichtete Gebäude erreichen schon seit alters her modernen Niedrigenergiestandard, und ein Gebäude aus Holz kann klimaneutral erbaut und nach dem Abbruch umweltschonend verwertet werden, da die pflanzliche Photosynthese das Kohlendioxid aus der Atmosphäre im Holz bindet.

Aufgrund seiner Entstehung durch Pflanzenwachstum ist Holz aber kein homogener Baustoff. Seine Eigenschaften längs und quer zur Faserrichtung können sehr stark voneinander abweichen. Dies gilt für die Wasseraufnahme ebenso wie für die statische Stabilität, für seine akustischen und thermischen Eigenschaften und für seine optische Anmutung. Auch innerhalb einer Holzart und selbst innerhalb eines Holzquerschnittes gibt es durch die Art der Entstehung große Unterschiede, die man bei der Verwendung genau beachten muss. Holz schwindet, es „arbeitet", es kann bei relativ niedriger Temperatur Feuer fangen. Auch die Schwächen des Holzes gehören untrennbar zu seinem Charakter.

Die Fortschritte in der Bautechnik haben auch zur Weiterentwicklung des Baustoffs Holz geführt. Der Einsatz von Leimen, Anstrichen und Beschichtungen gleicht die naturgemäßen Schwächen des Holzes gezielt aus und ist aus der heutigen Verwendung von Holz kaum mehr wegzudenken. Häufig wird gar nicht mehr Vollholz verwendet, sondern mehrschichtig verleimte Platten, synthetische Trägermaterialien mit einer Holzoberfläche oder Holzwerkstoffplatten unterschiedlichster Zusammensetzung. Die Innovationsfähigkeit des Menschen im Bereich der Holztechnik scheint keine Grenzen zu kennen.

Die heute oft gewünschte Bündigkeit und Fugenlosigkeit wird jedoch mit Holz kaum je zu erreichen sein. Die Abmessungen jeder Form von Bauholz sind enger begrenzt als die anderer Baustoffe. Konstruktionen aus Holz müssen nach wie vor aus einzelnen Elementen „gefügt" werden. Daher muss der Architekt mit Holz grundsätzlich präzise konstruieren und eine durchdachte Detaillierung finden. Dabei kann er sich jedoch häufig die alten, überlieferten Techniken und Erfahrungen zunutze machen.

Heute ist der Baustoff Holz häufig Bewährungsprobe und Testlabor junger, noch weithin unbekannter Architekten, da er verhältnismäßig preiswert ist und seine Bearbeitung vergleichsweise geringe Kosten verursacht. Geringere Baukosten erhöhen den

Spielraum für Experimente. Bauten aus Holz werden meist in der Werkstatt gefertigt; sie können dann relativ einfach in Teilen auch an abgelegene Orte transportiert und dort innerhalb kurzer Zeit montiert werden.

Angesichts seiner unbestreitbaren Vorzüge ist Holz jedoch im Begriff, sein Image als billiger Baustoff zu verlieren, da es gegenüber vielen synthetisch hergestellten Baumaterialien den Vorteil der Dauerhaftigkeit und Beständigkeit bietet. Holz verzeiht keine konstruktiven Fehler und keine Entscheidungen, die dem Gesetz der Logik und der Einfachheit zuwiderlaufen. Eine undurchdachte, aktuellen Moden folgende Detaillierung, die den notwendigen konstruktiven Holzschutz außer Acht lässt, wird das Holz, wenn es der Witterung ausgesetzt ist, schnell unansehnlich erscheinen lassen. Dauerhaft eindringende Feuchtigkeit führt zu Verfaulung und zum Schädlingsbefall. Am Umgang mit dem Baustoff Holz erkennt man bei heutigen Architekten, was sie wirklich zu leisten vermögen.

Wer aber die natürlichen Eigenschaften des Holzes kennt und nutzt, der hat einen wunderbar vielseitigen Werkstoff, der in der Hand des kreativen Entwerfers und Konstrukteurs zum Leben erwacht. Die Wandlungsfähigkeit und Anpassungsfähigkeit, die Holz erst zu einem „menschlichen" Baustoff machen, sind sichtbares Zeichen und vornehmste Eigenschaften des Holzes. Jede Lichtstimmung, jedes Wetter, jede Jahreszeit wird vom Holz widergespiegelt. Das Holz altert, zeigt Charakter und lässt, ein gewisses Maß an bewahrender Pflege vorausgesetzt, Geschichte ablesbar werden.

Besondere Ausdruckskraft entfaltet das Holz im Zusammenspiel mit anderen Materialien. Es kann je nach seiner Verwendung rau und ungehobelt wirken oder gleich einem präzise gefertigten Möbel die Hand schmeicheln, es kann Härte ausstrahlen oder seine haptischen Qualitäten ausspielen. Eine vielfach gebrochene, raue Oberfläche kann es durch seine Wärme und Glätte kontrastieren, eine glatte, fugenlose Oberfläche mit seiner lebendigen, organischen Struktur veredeln. Es kann in Abhängigkeit von seiner Umgebung feingliedrig, vergänglich und leicht oder auch massiv, robust und lastend wirken. Natürlich belassene und in kräftigen Farben lasierte oder gestrichene Holzoberflächen steigern einander in ihrer Wirkung. Bei Gebäuden, die in Naturlandschaften entstehen, wird Holz wie selbstverständlich als Baustoff eingesetzt, schmiegt es sich doch harmonisch seinem Umfeld an. Der gezielte flächige Einsatz industriell gefertigter Holzwerkstoffe, wie zum Beispiel unterschiedlicher Spanplatten, führt im urbanen Kontext zu reizvollen Effekten und bisher nicht möglichen Anwendungen.

Die aktuellen Projekte, die Holz als eine gestalterische Herausforderung begreifen, stellen immer wieder die Frage nach der richtigen Form, nach der einfachen Lösung, nach der logischen Antwort. Sie tun dies immer wieder auf ihre Weise und in ihrem eigenen Kontext, weshalb sie auch zunächst so unterschiedlich erscheinen. Sie alle haben jedoch eine Gemeinsamkeit: Immer stellt das sichtbar verwendete Holz das Bauwerk in einen Bezug zum Menschen, der es benutzt oder betrachtet.

Exteriors
Extérieurs
Außenansichten

Bar House

New York, NY, United States, 2005
Peter L. Gluck and Partners Architects
Photos © Paul Warchol

This large, one-family dwelling is situated in a valley. In winter, sunlight only reaches the bottom of the valley from the south. In contrast to the surrounding houses, this elongated building is therefore built at a right angle to the valley in order to make the most of the sun's angle. The rooms on the top floor therefore also face the South, offering the best views of the valley. Seen from the living room, which is glazed on three sides, we experience the house as an architectural promenade. The open roof terrace, where one can enjoy magnificent panoramic views, can be reached via an inside staircase and an outside flight of stairs running along the north side of the building. The building's façade is clad in tropical ipé wood in a warm shade of brown, while Wengé and sycamore were used for the fixtures and fittings in the light-filled interior. A smaller building, also clad in wood, houses a garage and a guest flat.

La grande maison individuelle est construite dans une vallée étroite dont en hiver le fond ne reçoit le soleil que côté plein sud. C'est pourquoi, à la différence des maisons environnantes, le bâtiment allongé est perpendiculaire à la vallée afin de tirer le meilleur parti possible de la lumière du soleil. C'est aussi pour cette raison que les pièces de l'étage sont orientées vers le sud, offrant par ailleurs la meilleure vue sur la vallée. Dès le salon, entièrement vitré sur trois côtés, la maison répond au concept de « promenade architecturale ». Un escalier intérieur et un autre extérieur longeant le côté nord permettent d'atteindre le toit en terrasse ouverte sur un splendide panorama. La façade du bâtiment est en bois tropical d'ipé au ton brun et chaud; les éléments de montage de l'intérieur, clair et lumineux, sont en wenge et en platane (sycomore). Un bâtiment plus petit, également habillé de bois, abrite un garage et un appartement pour héberger les hôtes.

Das Einfamilienhaus ist in einem engen Tal gelegen. Im Winter gelangt das Sonnenlicht nur direkt von Süden zur Talsohle. Im Gegensatz zu den umliegenden Häusern ist das lang gestreckte Gebäude daher rechtwinklig zum Tal gebaut, um so den Einfall des Sonnenlichtes optimal auszunutzen. Die Räume im Obergeschoss sind aus diesem Grund ebenfalls nach Süden ausgerichtet und bieten so auch den besten Blick auf das Tal. Ausgehend von dem an drei Seiten vollständig verglasten Wohnraum wirkt das Haus wie eine architektonische Promenade. Über eine Innentreppe und eine an der Nordseite verlaufende Außentreppe erreicht man die offene Dachterrasse, auf der sich ein prächtiger Rundblick genießen lässt. Die Fassade des Gebäudes besteht aus tropischem Ipé-Holz in einem warmen Braunton, für die Einbauten im licht und hell wirkenden Inneren wurden Wenge und Platane (Sycamore) verwendet. Ein kleineres, ebenfalls holzverkleidetes Gebäude beherbergt Garage und Gästewohnung.

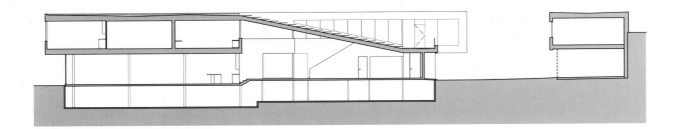

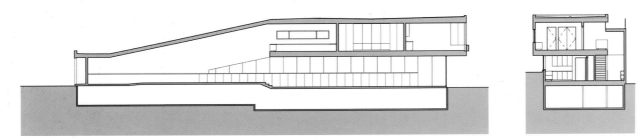

Sections · Sections · Schnitte

This house, whose façade is covered in tropical ipé wood, was designed as an architectural promenade leading from the fully-glazed living room on the ground floor to the roof terrace.

La maison revêtue de bois tropical d'ipé est conçue telle une « promenade architecturale », du salon entièrement vitré du rez-de-chaussée au toit en terrasse.

Das mit einer Fassade aus tropischem Ipé-Holz verkleidete Haus ist als architektonische Promenade konzipiert, die vom vollständig verglasten Wohnraum im Erdgeschoss bis zur Dachterrasse führt.

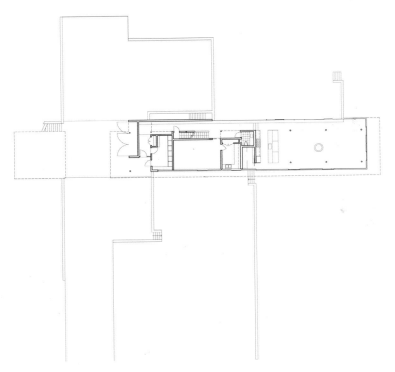

Ground floor · Rez-de-chaussée · Erdgeschoss

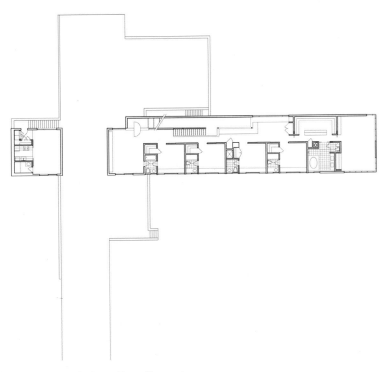

First floor · Premier étage · Erstes Obergeschoss

Cury House

São Paulo, Brazil, 2006
Marcio Kogan
Photos © Leonardo Finotti

Interior and exterior spaces at the Cury House merge almost seamlessly. An entrance patio leads via a generous living room to the minimalist garden. To the side, behind a quarrystone wall, is a narrow wing housing the kitchen and dining room. The living room is spanned by a free-standing frame that accommodates the private rooms. Above this is another small storey with an intimate retreat area. The material, and the very precise way of working it, is the focus of this design. The grey-brown natural stone wall running through the whole house is combined with the untreated wood of the terrace and an elongated pool in the outside area and with a light natural stone floor in the interior. With their white-plastered ceilings and walls, the rooms appear to be floating, and the vast sliding doors create transparency. Everywhere in the house, specially-designed building elements and wooden furniture are cleverly placed to structure the fluid space.

Les espaces intérieur et extérieur de la Cury House se fondent l'un dans l'autre presque sans transition. Le patio de l'entrée mène à un vaste salon qui touche au jardin minimaliste. Une aile latérale étroite, derrière un mur en moellons, abrite la cuisine et la salle à manger. Le salon est recouvert, sans appuis, par un autre corps de bâtiment où se trouvent les espaces privés. Au-dessus, un autre étage de taille réduite accueille un lieu de retraite intime. Le matériau très finement travaillé est au cœur du projet. Le mur de pierres naturelles gris-brun qui traverse toute la maison et se prolonge sur la terrasse, est associé, à l'extérieur, au bois non traité de la terrasse et à un bassin allongé, et à l'intérieur, au sol de pierres claires. Les murs et les plafonds enduits de blanc donnent l'impression que les pièces flottent, tandis que les immenses portes coulissantes veillent à la transparence. Partout, des éléments de construction et des meubles en bois spécialement conçus sont savamment placés pour structurer l'espace fluide.

Im Cury House gehen Innen- und Außenraum fast schwellenlos ineinander über. Ein Patio als Eingangsbereich leitet über in einen großzügigen Wohnraum, an den sich der minimalistisch gestaltete Garten anschließt. Seitlich liegt hinter einer Bruchsteinmauer ein schmaler Trakt mit Küche und Essraum. Der Wohnraum wird ohne Stützen von einem Körper überspannt, der die privaten Räume aufnimmt. Darüber befindet sich ein weiteres kleines Geschoss mit einem intimen Rückzugsbereich. Das Material und seine sehr präzise Verarbeitung stehen im Mittelpunkt dieses Entwurfs. Die das ganze Haus innen wie außen durchlaufende Mauer aus grau-braunem Naturstein wird im Außenbereich abwechslungsreich mit dem unbehandelten Holz der Terrasse und einem lang gestreckten Wasserbecken kombiniert, im Inneren mit einem Boden aus hellem Naturstein. Weiß verputzte Decken und Wände lassen die Räume wie schwebend wirken, und die gewaltigen Schiebetüren sorgen für Transparenz. Überall im Haus werden eigens entworfene Bauelemente und Möbel aus Holz gezielt eingesetzt, um den fließenden Raum zu strukturieren.

24

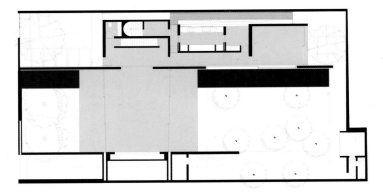

Ground floor · Rez-de-chaussée · Erdgeschoss

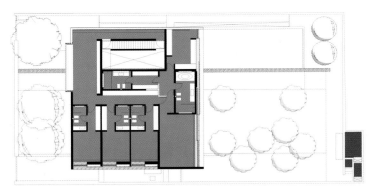

First floor · Premier étage · Erstes Obergeschoss

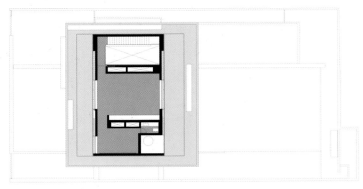

Second floor · Deuxième étage · Zweites Obergeschoss

The continuous natural stone wall divides the building into two parts. Its rough texture is a deliberate contrast to the precise details of the house.

Le mur continu en pierres naturelles divise le bâtiment en deux. Sa texture brute contraste volontairement avec la précision des détails qui règne dans la maison.

Die durchlaufende Natursteinwand teilt das Gebäude in zwei Teile. Ihre rohe Struktur steht in bewusstem Kontrast zur präzisen Detaillierung des Hauses.

Ridgewood House

Los Angeles, United States, 2006
David Thompson, Assembledge
Photos © Michael Weschler

The design for Ridgewood House was influenced by the style of classical modern architects such as Schindler and Neutra, who are famous for the houses they designed in Los Angeles. The simple cube and flying roof are the hallmarks of these modern architectural icons. This detached house, which is built on a corner plot, is entered via a raised front garden, which effectively sets the dwelling (conceived as a wooden cube) on a plinth. In order to make optimum use of the limited space, the garden was partly created on the roof of the lower-level garage and protected from the street by a wood-clad balustrade. This creates an interesting, rising series of rooms and outdoor spaces. The cube dwelling is covered with horizontal cedarwood boards, in contrast to the stucco in the living room, the colourfully coated plywood boards on the garage and the ipé wood on the terraces. Large panes of glass in the living room and on the top floor all but wipe away the border between inner and outer space.

Le concept de Ridgewood House est marqué par le style d'architectes modernes classiques tels Schindler et Neutra, dont les maisons de Los Angeles sont entrées dans l'histoire. Le cube lumineux et son toit à une seule pente renvoient clairement aux icônes de l'architecture moderne. Pour pénétrer dans la maison individuelle située sur un terrain d'angle, on traverse un jardinet surélevé qui place pour ainsi dire le cube de bois sur un socle. Afin d'exploiter au mieux l'espace réduit, le jardin occupe en partie le toit du garage construit à un niveau plus bas, isolé de la rue par une balustrade revêtue de bois, ce qui donne une succession intéressante de pièces et espaces libres en pente ascendante. Le cube d'habitation est recouvert de planches horizontales en cèdre qui contraste avec l'enduit lisse et blanc du salon, les panneaux de contreplaqué colorés du garage et le bois d'ipé des terrasses. Les grandes surfaces vitrées du salon et de l'étage gomment le passage de l'intérieur à l'extérieur pour former un espace continu fluide.

Der Entwurf für Ridgewood House ist geprägt vom Stil der Architekten der klassischen Moderne, wie Schindler und Neutra, die mit ihren Häusern in Los Angeles Geschichte geschrieben haben. Der klare Kubus und das Flugdach verweisen auf die Ikonen der modernen Architektur. Das auf einem Eckgrundstück errichtete Einfamilienhaus wird über einen erhöhten Vorgarten betreten, der das als hölzernen Kubus konzipierte Wohnhaus gewissermaßen auf einen Sockel stellt. Um den beschränkten Platz optimal auszunutzen, wurde der Garten teilweise auf dem Dach der niedriger gebauten Garage angelegt und mit einer holzverkleideten Brüstung gegen die Straße abgeschirmt, wodurch eine interessante, ansteigende Abfolge unterschiedlicher Räume und Freibereiche entstand. Der Kubus des Wohnhauses ist mit horizontal verlaufenden Brettern aus Zedernholz verkleidet, das mit weißem Glattputz im Wohnbereich, farbig beschichteten Sperrholzplatten an der Garage und Ipé-Holz auf den Terrassen kontrastiert wird. Große Glasflächen im Wohnbereich und im Obergeschoss lassen Innen- und Außenraum fließend ineinander übergehen.

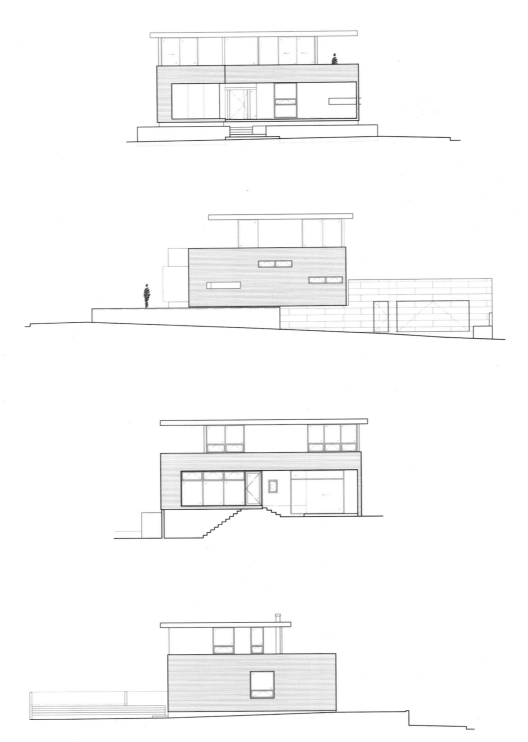

Elevations · Élévations · Aufrisse

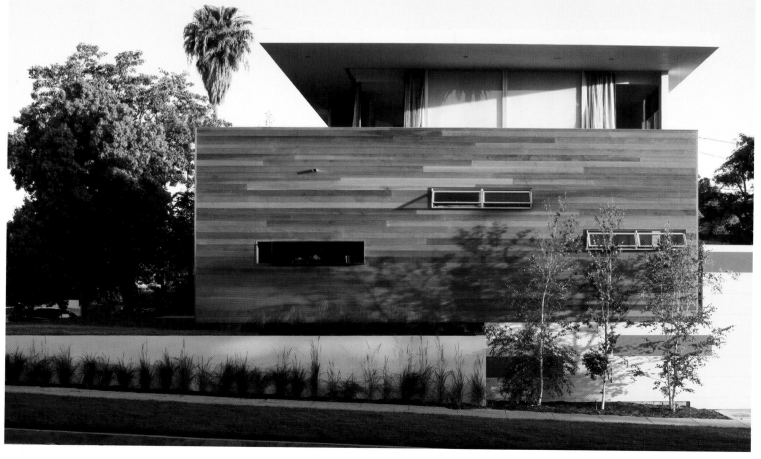

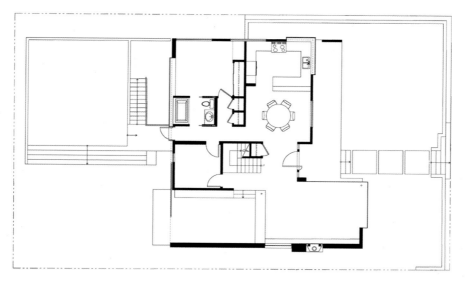

Ground floor · Rez-de-chaussée · Erdgeschoss

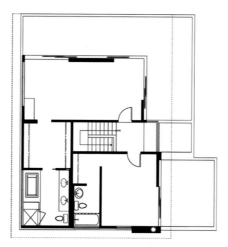

First floor · Premier étage · Erstes Obergeschoss

The use of wood and the abundant daylight create a cosy atmosphere.

La présence du bois et la lumière du jour qui pénètre librement dans la maison y créent une agréable atmosphère ambiante.

Durch die Verwendung von Holz und das ungehindert einfallende Tageslicht entsteht eine wohnliche Atmosphäre.

S401 House

Bragança Paulista, Brazil, 2006
Marcio Kogan
Photos © Nelson Kon

The S401 House displays elements of both an urban atrium house and a generous country house. Almost hermetically sealed from the outside by a wonderful natural stone wall, life in the house is organised around a large patio, which features tropical trees and bushes. All the rooms in the U-shaped layout are aligned with this patio. The crown of the house is the living room, which can be opened up or closed on two sides as needed with wooden sliding doors, which can be completely sunk into the walls. On the covered terrace, which is situated in front of this living room and extends to the patio, there are massive, untreated wooden seats designed by Carlos Motta. From here, a gallery with wooden walls and ceilings runs around the entire house, serving as a filter to the patio and providing access to all the rooms of the house, which can be separated from one another by wooden sliding doors or curtains.

La construction présente à la fois les éléments d'une maison de ville à patio et ceux d'une vaste maison de campagne. Presque hermétiquement isolée de l'extérieur par un magnifique mur de pierres naturelles, la vie s'y déroule autour du grand patio meublé de plantes et d'arbrisseaux tropicaux sur lequel donnent toutes les pièces de l'ensemble en U. Au sommet de la maison se trouve le salon qui peut être largement ouvert par des portes coulissantes en bois des deux côtés, ou fermé au besoin. Ces portes sont entièrement dissimulées dans les murs. Sur la terrasse couverte, qui précède le salon vers le patio, sont disposés des fauteuils en bois de Carlos Motta à l'aspect massif et brut. Une galerie aux murs et plafonds en bois part de la terrasse et fait le tour de la maison, tel un sas vers le patio, et donne accès aux pièces des ailes de la maison, séparées les unes des autres par des portes coulissantes en bois ou des rideaux.

Das Haus S401 weist sowohl Elemente des städtischen Atriumhauses als auch die eines großzügigen Landhauses auf. Nach außen mittels einer prächtigen Natursteinwand fast hermetisch abgeschlossen, organisiert sich das Leben im Haus um den großen, mit tropischen Bäumen und Stauden gestalteten Patio. Alle Räume des im Grundriss U-förmigen Hauses sind auf diesen Patio ausgerichtet. Im Scheitelpunkt des Hauses befindet sich der Wohnraum, der mit Schiebetüren aus Holz zu beiden Seiten des Grundstücks weit geöffnet oder nach Bedarf geschlossen werden kann. Die Schiebetüren lassen sich vollkommen in den Wänden versenken. Auf der überdeckten Terrasse, die vor diesem Wohnbereich zum Patio hin gelegen ist, stehen massige, roh wirkende Holzsessel von Carlos Motta. Von hier aus läuft eine Galerie mit Wänden und Decken aus Holz rund um das gesamte Haus, die wie ein Filter zum Patio hin fungiert und über die die Räume in den Flügeln des Hauses erreicht werden können. Diese Räume lassen sich mit Holz-Schiebetüren oder textilen Vorhängen voneinander abtrennen.

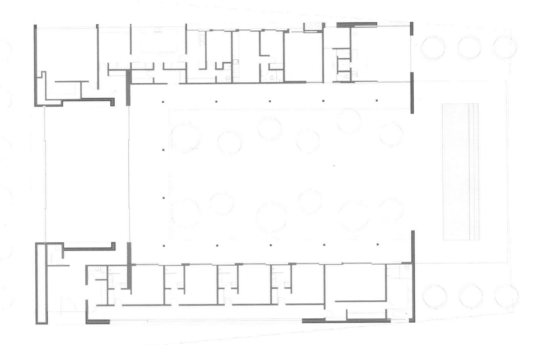

Plan · Plan · Grundriss

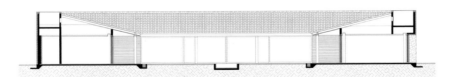

Section · Section · Schnitt

On the back wall of the living room, which can be opened on the sides with solid wood sliding doors, there is a sturdy open fireplace echoing the horizontal lines of the house.

Contre le fronton du salon, que de massives portes coulissantes en bois permettent d'ouvrir complètement sur ses longs côtés, une immense cheminée poursuit le tracé horizontal de la maison.

An der Stirnwand des Wohnraums, der sich an den Längsseiten durch massive Holzschiebetüren vollständig öffnen lässt, steht ein mächtiger offener Kamin, der die horizontale Linienführung des Hauses reflektiert.

Müller Gritsch House

Lenzburg, Switzerland, 2007
Andreas Fuhrimann Gabrielle Hächler Architects
Photos © Valentin Jeck

This house-cum-studio for an artist couple was built over an existing cellar on a garden plot. The large space allocation plan, which comprises the two workshops, a living room with an open-plan kitchen, two bedrooms and a guest room, could only be financed by resorting to prefabricated wooden parts. The two 3.4-metre-high studios were arranged on top of each other, and the one-and-a-half storey living room forms the focal point of the house. Here the central core from which the house unfolds is an open fireplace and a staircase. The studios are each directly linked to the living room, but they can also be separated, if necessary, to allow the artists to work undisturbed. In the design, particular attention was paid to the direction of sunlight, which adds to the striking impact of the room. To cover the walls and ceilings, the architects used chipboard with a smooth, low-key appearance. Spruce was used on the exterior, but cement fibreboards were added for fire protection and structural stability.

Cette maison-atelier d'un couple d'artistes a été érigée sur une cave. Seul le recours à des éléments de bois préfabriqués a permis de financer les nombreuses pièces, dont deux ateliers, un salon et une cuisine ouverte, deux chambres à coucher et des chambres d'amis. Les deux ateliers d'une hauteur de plafond de 3,40 m se trouvent l'un au-dessus de l'autre. À partir du salon, qui constitue le cœur de la maison sur un étage et demi, l'habitation se déploie autour d'un noyau central formé par la cheminée et l'escalier. Les ateliers donnent sur le salon, mais peuvent en être séparés pour permettre à leurs occupants de travailler en paix. Les concepteurs ont accordé un soin particulier à l'éclairage qui contribue à l'effet surprenant de cet espace original. Pour habiller les murs et les plafonds, les architectes ont choisi des panneaux de contreplaqué qui donnent une impression d'étendue et de calme. À l'extérieur, on a posé de l'épicéa, mais aussi des panneaux de fibres de ciment pour des raisons de protection contre l'incendie et de physique des bâtiments.

Das Atelierhaus für ein Künstlerpaar wurde auf einem bestehenden Keller eines Gartengrundstücks errichtet. Das große Raumprogramm, das zwei Ateliers, einen Wohnraum mit offener Küche, zwei Schlafzimmer und Gästezimmer umfasste, war nur durch den Rückgriff auf vorfabrizierte Holzelemente zu finanzieren. Die beiden 3,40 m hohen Ateliers wurden übereinander angeordnet, den Mittelpunkt des Hauses bildet der eineinhalbgeschossige Wohnraum. Von ihm ausgehend entwickelt sich das Haus um einen zentralen Kern, der aus einem offenen Kamin und der Treppe besteht. Die Ateliers haben jeweils eine direkte Verbindung zum Wohnraum, sie sind jedoch bei Bedarf auch abtrennbar, um ungestörtes Arbeiten zu ermöglichen. Besondere Aufmerksamkeit wurde beim Entwurf des Hauses der Lichtführung geschenkt, die die spannungsvolle Raumwirkung zusätzlich unterstützt. Zur Verkleidung von Wänden und Decken verwendeten die Architekten Spanplatten mit einer flächigen und ruhigen Anmutung. Außen wurde Fichtenholz eingesetzt, aus Gründen des Brandschutzes oder der Bauphysik wurden zusätzlich Zementfaserplatten angebracht.

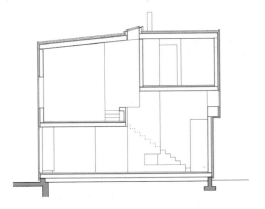

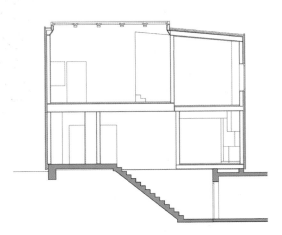

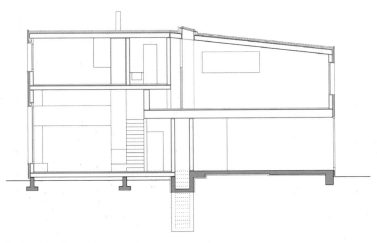

Sections · Sections · Schnitte

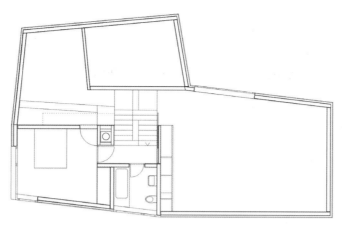

Basement · Sous-sol · Kellergeschoss

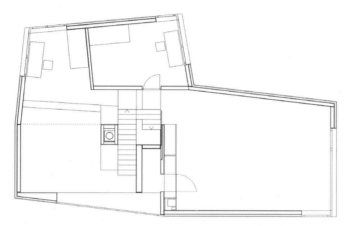

Ground floor · Rez-de-chaussée · Erdgeschoss

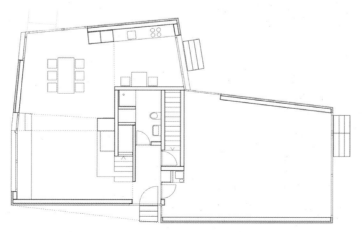

First floor · Premier étage · Erstes Obergeschoss

Flooded House

Kuruçeşme, Istanbul, Turkey, 2003
GAD Architecture-Gokhan Avcioglu
Photos © Ali Bekman

This house, which is situated in a protected zone on the Bosphorus, is similar to a previous house preserved in several photographs in the state archive. The architects' design aimed to harmonise the traditional typology of a house built on the water with modern needs. The sandalwood façade, the wooden window frames and the flat sloping roof with its wide overhang follow the historical model. In contrast to the previous building, the steeply sloping ground leading to the water was excavated to add three extra storeys and create space for a swimming pool in the garden. There is another swimming pool inside the house. By building two swimming pools, the architects aimed to reinterpret the traditional shape of the Ottoman boathouse, and this is aptly reflected in the project's name: "Flooded House". The wood used throughout the house contrasts with the smooth exposed concrete, the greenish natural stone tiles and the dry-stone walls.

Située dans un site protégé du Bosphore, la maison est inspirée d'un bâtiment précédent dont on trouve quelques photographies aux Archives nationales. Le projet des architectes visait à concilier la typologie traditionnelle d'une maison au bord de l'eau et les exigences de la modernité. Si la façade en bois de santal, les fenêtres en bois et le toit plat incliné à large avancée évoquent le modèle historique, la pente très raide qui descend vers l'eau a été obtenue par excavation du terrain pour ajouter trois étages au bâtiment et faire place à un bassin de natation dans le jardin. Une autre piscine se trouve à l'intérieur. Avec ces deux pièces d'eau, les architectes ont cherché à réinterpréter la forme traditionnelle de la maison-bateau ottomane, comme en témoigne notamment le nom du projet, « Flooded House » (la maison inondée). Le bois utilisé dans toute la maison contraste avec du béton apparent coffré et lisse, des dalles de pierres naturelles verdâtres et une maçonnerie de moellons secs.

Das in einer Landschaftsschutzzone am Bosporus gelegene Haus ist einem Vorgängerbau nachempfunden, von dem sich einige Fotografien in einem Staatlichen Archiv befinden. Der Entwurf der Architekten zielte darauf ab, die traditionelle Typologie eines am Wasser errichteten Hauses mit modernen Anforderungen in Einklang zu bringen. Während die Fassade aus Sandelholz, die Holzfenster und das flach geneigte Dach mit breitem Dachüberstand das historische Vorbild zitieren, wird das sehr steil zum Wasser hin abfallende Gelände durch Erdabtragungen genutzt, um im Vergleich zum ursprünglichen Gebäude drei zusätzliche Geschosse einzuziehen und Raum für ein Schwimmbecken im Garten zu schaffen. Ein weiterer Swimming Pool befindet sich im Inneren des Hauses. Die Architekten beabsichtigten durch den Einbau von zwei Schwimmbecken, die überlieferte Form des ottomanischen Bootshauses neu zu interpretieren, was sich nicht zuletzt im Projektnamen „Flooded House" niederschlägt. Das überall im Haus verwendete Holz wird mit glatt geschaltem Sichtbeton, grünlichen Natursteinplatten und trocken vermauertem Bruchstein kontrastiert.

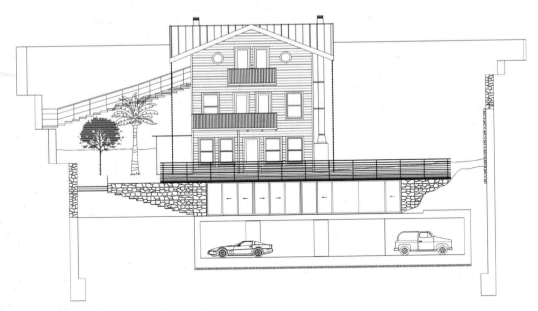

Front elevation · Élévation frontale · Vorderansicht

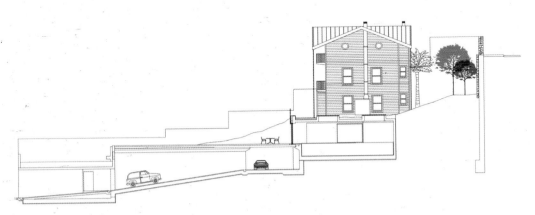

Rear elevation · Élévation arrière · Hinteransicht

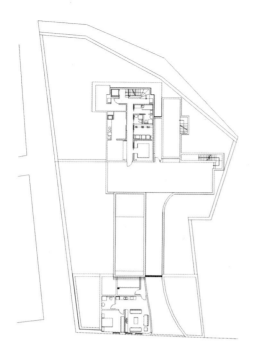

Basement · Sous-sol · Kellergeschoss

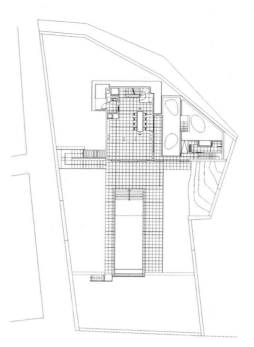

Lower level · Niveau inférieur · Untere Ebene

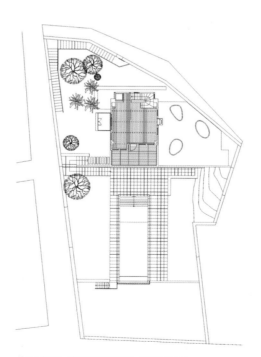

Upper level · Niveau supérieur · Obere Ebene

The swimming pool, directly adjacent to the living area, receives natural light through the organic forms of the skylights.

La lumière du jour tombe dans le bassin qui jouxte la partie habitable par des ouvertures aux formes organiques percées dans le toit.

In das direkt an den Wohnbereich angrenzende Schwimmbecken fällt durch organisch geformte Dachfenster natürliches Licht.

The Avenel House

Central Victoria, Australia, 2006
Paul Morgan Architects
Photos © John Gollings

This building lies on an expansive plot of land in a rural, sparsely populated area of the state of Victoria characterised by intense sunlight and strong winds. The generous glass panels in the living room provide sweeping views of the countryside. The roof offers a protective cover to the entire building and appears to envelop it at the same time. A large overhang also protects the large glass surfaces from the beating sun. Horizontal wooden slats shade the windows on the narrow side of the house. The principal materials used to build the house are concrete and a greyish-brown granite that was quarried on the plot. The floors in the living area are made from Australian brushbox wood, while the terrace is covered with tropical merbau.

Le bâtiment occupe un vaste terrain dans la partie rurale peu peuplée de l'État de Victoria. Le paysage y est marqué par l'intensité du soleil et la force du vent. Cependant, les grandes surfaces vitrées du salon offrent une large vue sur les environs. Le toit protecteur recouvre tout le volume du bâtiment qu'il semble envelopper. Une large avancée protège les vitres du soleil de midi. Les fenêtres des petits côtés de la maison sont ombragées par des lamelles horizontales de bois dur. Pour le gros-œuvre, on a utilisé comme principaux matériaux le béton et un granit gris-brun présent sur le terrain. Les planchers de l'habitation sont en brushbox, une essence australienne, tandis que la terrasse est en bois tropical de merbau.

Das Gebäude liegt auf einem weitläufigen Grundstück im ländlichen, dünn besiedelten Teil des Bundesstaats Victoria. Die Landschaft ist geprägt von intensiver Sonneneinstrahlung und starkem Wind. Dennoch eröffnen die großzügigen Glasflächen des Wohnbereichs einen weiten Blick über die Landschaft. Das Dach legt sich schützend über das gesamte Bauvolumen und scheint es gleichsam einzuhüllen. Eine weite Auskragung schützt dabei die großen Glasflächen vor der hoch stehenden Sonne. Die Fenster an den Schmalseiten des Hauses werden durch horizontale Hartholzlamellen verschattet. Die für den Bau des Hauses im Wesentlichen benutzten Materialien sind Beton und ein auf dem Grundstück vorkommender grau-brauner Granit. Die Fußböden im Wohnbereich bestehen aus australischem Brushbox-Holz, die Terrasse ist mit tropischem Merbau belegt.

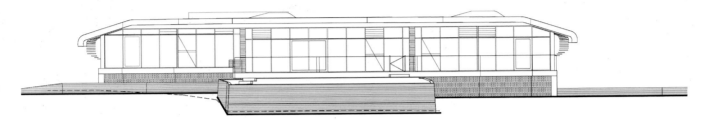

Front elevation · Élévation frontale · Vorderansicht

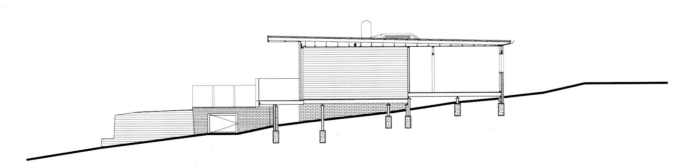

Side elevation · Élévation latérale · Seitenansicht

The fantastic panoramic view over the countryside largely determined the design of the house. The terrace is bordered by a completely transparent balustrade made of shatter-proof glass.

La vue panoramique grandiose sur le paysage environnant a largement déterminé le concept de la maison. La terrasse est entourée d'une balustrade entièrement transparente en verre incassable.

Der großartige Panoramablick über die Landschaft bestimmte in hohem Maße den Entwurf des Hauses. Die Terrasse ist mit einer völlig transparenten Brüstung aus bruchsicherem Glas eingefasst.

Lengau Lodge

Limpopo Province, South Africa, 2004
DRY Design Inc
Photos © Undine Prohl

Lengau Lodge lies in the middle of the 16,000 km² Welgevonden nature reserve, in the South African province of Limpopo. The complex consists of a total of nine buildings whose arrangement was determined by the natural gradient of the land. Ecology and sustainability were the essential starting points for the design. For example, care was taken not to remove excavated material from the site and, as a point of principle, to use stones found on the site to pave the paths and for the landscaping. The gabled roofs are thatched with locally sourced straw, and the flat roofs are decorated with grasses from the region. The buildings do not have air conditioning. Verandas supply shade, while clerestories arranged above them allow light to penetrate the buildings. Solid walls store heat and release it in the cooler seasons. In addition to concrete floors and brick walls, wooden building parts are the central elements of the individual houses, such as the wooden truss for the gabled roof, which has deliberately been left visible.

Lengau Lodge est situé au cœur des 16 000 km² du parc naturel de Welgevonden, dans la province sud-africaine du Limpopo. L'ensemble se compose de neuf bâtiments au total, dont l'orientation est déterminée par les variations naturelles du terrain. Écologie et durabilité ont été les principales lignes directrices du projet. On a notamment veillé à ne pas évacuer les déblais et à utiliser principalement les pierres trouvées sur place pour paver les chemins et aménager le paysage. Les toits à deux pentes sont recouverts de paille d'origine locale, les toits plats sont, eux, plantés d'herbes de la région. Les bâtiments ne sont pas climatisés artificiellement. Des vérandas apportent de l'ombre, tandis que la rangée de fenêtres percées laisse entrer la lumière jusqu'au fond de la maison. Les murs épais emmagasinent la chaleur et la restituent à la saison fraîche. Avec le béton du sol et les murs maçonnés, les éléments de construction en bois jouent un rôle central dans les maisons, telle la charpente visible du toit.

Lengau Lodge liegt inmitten des 16.000 km² großen Naturschutzgebiets Welgevonden in der südafrikanischen Provinz Limpopo. Die Anlage besteht aus insgesamt neun Gebäuden, deren Ausrichtung durch den natürlichen Geländeverlauf bestimmt wird. Ökologie und Nachhaltigkeit waren wesentliche Ausgangspunkte des Entwurfs. So wurde beispielsweise darauf geachtet, Aushub nicht vom Gelände abzufahren und grundsätzlich die vor Ort gefundenen Gesteine für die Pflasterung von Wegen und die Landschaftsgestaltung zu verwenden. Die Satteldächer sind mit Stroh, das vor Ort gewonnen wurde, gedeckt, die Flachdächer mit aus der Region stammenden Gräsern begrünt. Die Bauten sind nicht künstlich klimatisiert. Veranden sorgen für Schatten, darüber angeordnete Obergaden lassen dennoch Licht tief in die Gebäude fallen. Massive Mauern speichern Wärme und geben sie in der kühlen Jahreszeit ab. Neben dem Beton für die Fußböden und den gemauerten Wänden sind Bauteile aus Holz zentrale Elemente der einzelnen Häuser, wie das hölzerne Tragwerk der Satteldächer, das man sichtbar belassen hat.

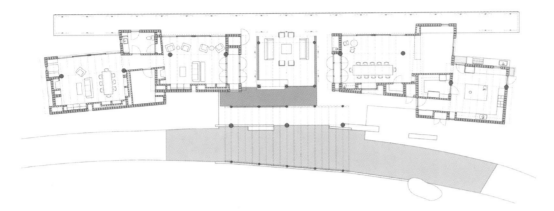

Plan · Plan · Grundriss

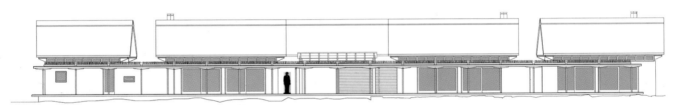

Front elevation · Élévation frontale · Vorderansicht

Side elevation · Élévation latérale · Seitenansicht

The construction blends in harmoniously with the countryside. Canopies provide sufficient shade, but the clerestory ensures that the inside remains bright.

L'ensemble s'intègre harmonieusement au paysage environnant. Les toits offrent une bonne protection contre le soleil, mais les intérieurs restent malgré tout clairs et lumineux grâce aux fenêtres de la partie supérieure.

Die Anlage fügt sich harmonisch in die Landschaft ein. Schutzdächer bieten ausreichend Schatten, dennoch sind die Innenräume dank der Obergaden licht und hell.

Grøndalen Apartments

Hemsedal, Norway, 2007
SKAARA Arkitekter AS
Photos © 360foto, Frank Tolpinrud

This apartment house is the first project to be finished as part of a master plan to develop the Solsiden ski resort. The elongated structure contains smaller split-level apartments on the lower floor, while the upper floor has five identical, two-storeyed apartments, each of which can be directly entered from the outside. All the apartments have generous, open living areas and terraces or covered loggias. The living areas' floors and walls are in light oak and deal. The façade consists of dark-stained deal. While the actual structure has wooden lagging consisting of wide horizontal bands with sturdy protruding beams, the entrance areas on the access side are covered with delicate, filigree-like horizontal strips. The roof is covered with untreated larch-wood boards.

Cette maison de plusieurs appartements est le premier projet achevé dans le cadre d'un plan-maître d'exploitation et de développement de la zone skiable de Solsiden. Le bâtiment allongé comprend à l'étage inférieur de petits appartements à demi-niveau et à l'étage supérieur cinq logements identiques en duplex avec un accès direct vers l'extérieur. Tous les appartements possèdent un vaste salon ouvert et des terrasses ou des loggias couvertes. Les sols et les murs des salons ont été laissés dans un bois de chêne et de sapin de teinte claire. La façade est en sapin teinté en brun sombre. Alors que le bâtiment proprement dit possède un coffrage fait de larges bandes horizontales et de solides lattes saillantes en bois, les entrées des appartements qui s'avancent du côté de l'accès principal sont enveloppées de fines baguettes horizontales à l'aspect filigrané. Le toit est couvert de plaques de mélèze non traité.

Das Apartmenthaus ist das erste fertig gestellte Projekt innerhalb eines Masterplans für die Erschließung und Entwicklung des Skigebiets Solsiden. Der längliche Baukörper enthält in der unteren Etage kleinere Split-Level-Apartments und in der oberen Etage fünf gleichartige, jeweils über zwei Etagen reichende Wohnungen, die einen direkten Zugang von außen haben. Alle Apartments verfügen über einen großzügigen, offenen Wohnbereich und Terrassen oder überdeckte Loggien. Die Fußböden und Wände der Wohnbereiche sind in hellem Eichen- und Tannenholz gehalten. Die Fassade besteht aus dunkel gebeiztem Tannenholz. Während der eigentliche Baukörper eine Holzverschalung in breiten horizontalen Bändern mit weit vorspringenden, kräftigen Leisten besitzt, werden die an der Zugangsseite vorgestellten Eingangsbereiche mit feinen horizontalen Leisten umhüllt, die sehr filigran wirken. Das Dach ist mit unbehandelten Lärchenholzplatten gedeckt.

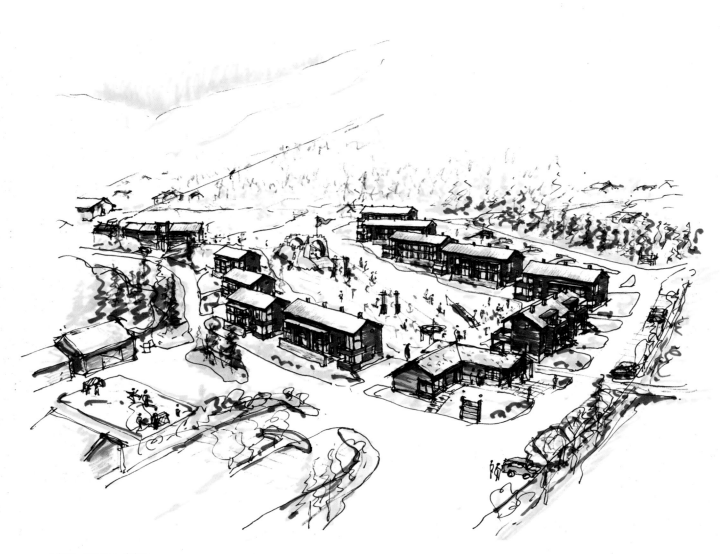

Sketch · Esquisse · Skizze

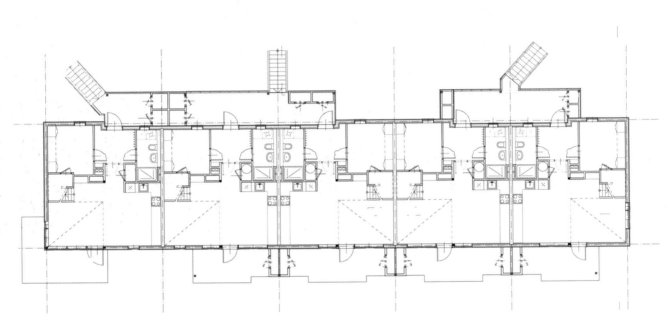

Plan · Plan · Grundriss

By using wood both for the interior and on the façade, the building completely blends in with its natural environment.

Le bois de l'intérieur et de la façade permet à la maison de s'intégrer parfaitement à la nature environnante.

Durch den Einsatz von Holz in den Innenräumen und an der Fassade passt sich das Gebäude seiner natürlichen Umgebung vollkommen an.

Haugsætra

Kvamsfjellet, Norway, 2002
SKAARA Arkitekter AS
Photos © Espen Grønli

When designing this house, the architects took their inspiration from the traditional chalets of the region to integrate the new building with its environment as harmoniously as possible. The elongated construction with a flat, slate-covered pitched roof is positioned to give sweeping views to the south and the west from the living room. The dining room was designed as a light, completely transparent glass box that slightly protrudes from the rest of the building. The eaves of the roof are also completely glazed in order to maximise light while protecting the wooden house from the harsh weather. This creates a covered outside path, which opens out onto a terrace at the end of the building. The building was conceived as a wooden house, and this can be clearly seen in the structure and the material used. The white-stained, delicately structured oak and pinewood inside contrast with the dark-stained, horizontally-arranged pinewood on the façade and with the natural stone masonry, some of it drystone.

Pour la conception de cette maison, les architectes se sont inspirés des cabanes traditionnelles de la région afin d'intégrer le nouveau bâtiment le plus harmonieusement possible à son environnement. La construction allongée au toit à deux pentes couvert d'ardoises est orientée de manière à ouvrir une large vue vers le sud et vers l'ouest depuis le salon. La salle à manger est un bloc de verre lumineux et parfaitement transparent qui dépasse légèrement du volume global. Pour protéger la maison en bois du climat rigoureux sans en assombrir l'intérieur, la partie inférieure du toit est elle aussi entièrement vitrée. Il en résulte un passage extérieur couvert qui s'élargit en une terrasse à l'extrémité du bâtiment. La maison est conçue en bois, comme en témoignent la structure et les matériaux utilisés. Le chêne et le pin finement structurés et teintés de blanc à l'intérieur s'opposent au pin teinté de brun sombre disposé horizontalement sur la façade ainsi qu'aux murs partiellement en pierres sèches.

Beim Entwurf des Hauses ließen sich die Architekten von den traditionellen Hütten der Region inspirieren, um den Neubau möglichst harmonisch in seine Umgebung einzufügen. Der längliche Baukörper mit flachem, schiefergedecktem Satteldach ist so ausgerichtet, dass sich vom Wohnbereich ein weiter Blick nach Süden und Westen öffnet. Der Essbereich ist als lichter, völlig transparenter Glaskasten gestaltet, der geringfügig aus dem Gebäudevolumen herausragt. Um die Belichtung nicht zu beeinträchtigen und dennoch das Holzhaus vor der rauen Witterung zu schützen, ist auch der Traufbereich des Daches vollständig verglast. Es entsteht ein überdachter, außen liegender Gang, der sich am Ende des Gebäudes zu einer Terrasse erweitert. Das Haus ist als Holzhaus konzipiert, was sich deutlich an der Struktur und dem eingesetzten Material ablesen lässt. Dem weiß gebeizten, fein strukturierten Eichen- und Kiefernholz im Inneren wird dunkel gebeiztes, horizontal verbautes Kiefernholz an der Außenfassade, teilweise auch trocken geschichtetes Natursteinmauerwerk, gegenübergestellt.

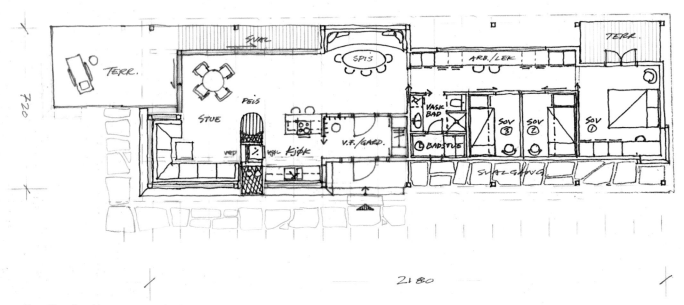

720

TERR.

SVAL

SPIS

ARB./LEK

TERR.

STUE

PEIS

VASK
BAD

SOV
③

SOV
②

SOV
①

VED

V.F./GARD.

KJØK

BADSTUE

SVALGANG

2180

Plan · Plan · Grundriss

Not only is the living and dining area comfortable and cosy, it also has wonderful views.

Le séjour avec un espace repas n'est pas seulement confortable et agréable à vivre, il offre aussi une vue splendide.

Der Wohn- und Essbereich besitzt nicht nur eine komfortable Wohnlichkeit, er bietet zudem eine wunderbare Aussicht.

Archipelago House

Stockholm, Sweden, 2006
Tham & Videgård Hansson Arkitekter
Photos © Ali Bekman

This country cottage, which is situated on an island full of pine trees in the sea off Stockholm, owes its structure first to its position between two towering rocky outcrops and, second, to the wonderful views of the sea. These contrasting aspects, determined by the natural landscape, are incorporated in the building and formed the leitmotif of the design theme. While the bedrooms and adjoining rooms were relegated to the back of the house, the living quarters occupy the entire large glazed front looking out over the water. The three-tier floor plan creates a charming perspective from room to room and triangular terraces that are sheltered from the wind. By using the sliding doors, these areas can be linked both spatially and functionally, creating unity between the inside and the outside. Wood is present throughout this light-filled house, which almost seems to float. Floors in white-oiled oak, ceiling and walls in white-painted pine, the window frames, the pergola and finally, the façade clad in dark-stained spruce plywood – they all demonstrate the possibilities of this material.

La maison d'été, érigée sur une île plantée de pins au large de Stockholm, doit sa structure à son emplacement entre deux blocs rocheux et à la vue merveilleuse sur la mer. La réunion de ces deux éléments naturels contrastants a tenu lieu de fil directeur pour la conception du bâtiment. Tandis que les chambres et les pièces attenantes sont en retrait, le salon occupe tout le vaste front vitré donnant sur la mer. Le décalage à angle droit sur trois plans, qui ouvre des perspectives pleines de charme d'une pièce à l'autre, a créé des terrasses triangulaires protégées du vent. Les portes coulissantes permettent de combiner ces espaces, aussi bien du point de vue spatial que fonctionnel, pour fusionner intérieur et extérieur. Dans cette maison légère qui semble flotter, le bois est omniprésent. Les planchers de chêne huilé blanc, les plafonds et les murs de pin blanc, les cadres de fenêtres, la pergola et la façade en contreplaqué d'épicéa teinté de brun sombre attestent des multiples possibilités d'utilisation de ce matériau.

Das Sommerhaus, auf einer kiefernbestandenen Insel vor Stockholm gelegen, bezieht seine Struktur zum einen aus der Lage zwischen zwei aufragenden Felsblöcken, zum anderen aus der wundervollen Aussicht auf das Meer. Diese durch die landschaftlichen Gegebenheiten bedingten kontrastierenden Aspekte sind in dem Gebäude aufgenommen und zum Thema des Entwurfs gemacht worden. Während die Schlaf- und Nebenräume zurückversetzt wurden, nehmen die Wohnräume die gesamte großflächig verglaste Front zum Wasser hin ein. Durch die dreifache Staffelung entstehen einerseits reizvolle Durchblicke von Raum zu Raum, andererseits windgeschützte dreieckige Terrassenbereiche. Mit Hilfe der Schiebetüren können sich diese Bereiche räumlich und funktional überlagern und somit Innen und Außen ineinander fließen. Holz, aus dem das leichte, fast schwebend wirkende Haus konstruiert ist, ist überall präsent. Fußböden aus weiß geöltem Eichenholz, die Decke und Wände aus weiß gestrichener Kiefer, die Fensterprofile, die hölzerne Pergola und schließlich die Fassadenbekleidung aus dunkel gebeiztem Fichtensperrholz demonstrieren die Möglichkeiten des Materials.

Elevation · Élévation · Aufriss

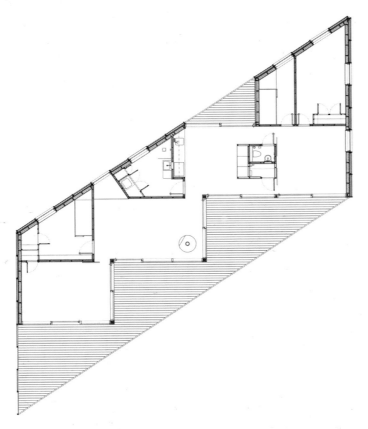

Plan · Plan · Grundriss

The triangular terraces in front of the living area provide protection from the wind and sun, while at the same time providing unobstructed views over the Baltic Sea.

Les terrasses triangulaires devant les pièces de séjour protègent du vent et du soleil, mais offrent aussi une vue parfaitement dégagée sur la mer Baltique.

Die dem Wohnbereich vorgelagerten dreieckigen Terrassen schützen vor Wind und Sonne, gewähren aber zugleich auch einen freien Blick auf die Ostsee.

Burrawang House

Burrawang, New South Wales, Australia, 2005
Whitcher Matyear Architects
Photos © Murray Fredericks

The basic shape of this house for a five-person family calls to mind the simple agricultural buildings of the district. However, the recesses in the cube form and the elegant façade create surprising and varied spatial connections. The large terrace, which can be used as a living room all year round and can therefore be seen as yet another room, was one of the owner-builder's main requirements. The dwelling was designed as a zero-energy house. It was therefore placed on the far southern edge of the plot, and the windows were made as large as possible in order to maximise sunlight from the north in the cool season. The deep, stone window ledge stores heat from the sun and releases it at night. Venetian blinds keep the summer heat out, and horizontal slats provide shade. The dark, shimmering hardwood floors inside the house were recovered from a demolished commercial building in Sydney and reused here.

La forme de base de cette maison, qui abrite une famille de cinq personnes, rappelle les modestes bâtiments agricoles de la région. Des coupes dans la cubature et la façade élégante y créent cependant des volumes surprenants et très variés. La grande terrasse, d'espace utilisable toute l'année, qui s'enfonce profondément dans le corps du bâtiment afin de former une pièce supplémentaire, était l'une des principales exigences du maître d'ouvrage. La maison répond au concept de l'habitation passive (à basse consommation énergétique). C'est pour cette raison qu'elle a été construite à l'extrémité sud du terrain et dotée de fenêtres les plus grandes possibles afin d'exploiter au maximum l'ensoleillement du nord pendant les mois d'hiver. Les profonds appuis de fenêtres maçonnés sont destinés à emmagasiner la chaleur pour la restituer pendant la nuit. En revanche, la chaleur de l'été est retenue par des stores mobiles et des lamelles horizontales procurant de l'ombre. Le bois dur à l'éclat sombre des planchers a été récupéré à Sydney dans un bâtiment qui avait été abattu.

Die Grundform des Hauses für eine fünfköpfige Familie orientiert sich an den einfachen landwirtschaftlichen Gebäuden der Gegend. Durch Einschnitte in die Kubatur und die raffinierte Fassadenlösung besitzt das Haus jedoch überraschende und abwechslungsreiche Raumbeziehungen. Die große Terrasse als ganzjährig nutzbarer Wohnraum, die tief in das Volumen reicht und so zu einem zusätzlichen Zimmer wird, war eine zentrale Vorgabe des Bauherrn. Das Wohnhaus ist als Passivhaus konzipiert. So wurde es weit an den südlichen Rand des Grundstücks platziert und die Fenster so groß wie möglich dimensioniert, um in der kühlen Jahreszeit die Sonneneinstrahlung von Norden zu maximieren. Die tiefe, gemauerte Fensterbank soll die Sonnenwärme speichern und sie in der Nacht wieder abstrahlen. Die Hitze des Sommers dagegen wird durch bewegliche Jalousien und horizontale, Schatten spendende Lamellen abgehalten. Der dunkel schimmernde Hartholzfußboden im Inneren wurde aus einem abgerissenen Gewerbebau in Sydney geborgen und wieder verwendet.

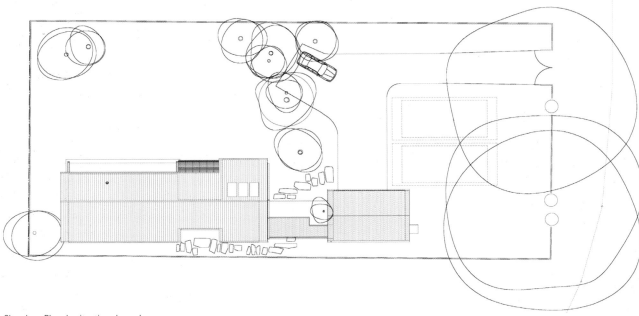

Site plan · Plan de situation · Lageplan

the summer months, the projecting roof prevents the intense sunlight from penetrating inside, while gentler rays are ltered by the horizontal slats.

endant les mois d'été, l'avancée profonde du toit empêche le soleil trop intense de pénétrer, tandis que les rayons obliques ont filtrés par les lamelles horizontales.

den Sommermonaten verhindert das weit vorspringende Dach das Eindringen der intensiven Sonneneinstrahlung, während e flacher auftreffenden Strahlen von den horizontalen Lamellen gefiltert werden.

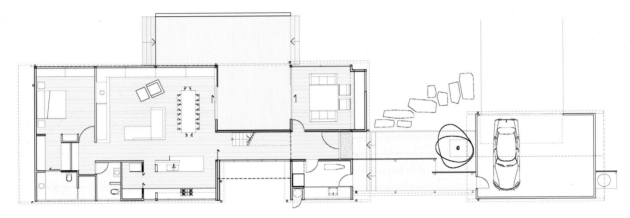

Ground floor · Rez-de-chaussée · Erdgeschoss

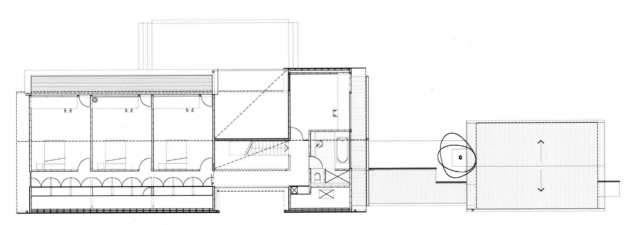

First floor · Premier étage · Erstes Obergeschoss

House K

Stockholm, Sweden, 2004
Tham & Videgård Hansson Arkitekter
Photos © Ali Bekman

This house in Stocksund was designed as a narrow block standing crosswise on the available plot of land and dividing it into a front area and a garden. The house is therefore virtually only visible from the front and resembles an inhabitable wall. The entrance and the staircase are combined in a box on the ground floor, while the individual rooms on the upper floor can be reached via a central corridor. Two-storey rooms allow diagonal perspectives every now and then and turn movement through the house into an interesting series of very different spatial impressions which the architects call "visual short-circuits". The house was built from in-situ concrete with permanent shuttering for insulation. The internal walls are plastered white, and all the floors and wooden details are made from ash. The façade consists of overlapping black-stained plywood boards.

Cette maison de Stocksund est conçue comme un bloc rectangulaire étroit posé transversalement au terrain disponible qu'elle divise en deux. Par conséquent, elle révèle son caractère de maison uniquement sur sa façade frontale et ressemble à un mur habitable. Au rez-de-chaussée ouvert, l'entrée et l'escalier forment un bloc, tandis qu'un couloir central dessert les différentes pièces de l'étage. Des espaces en duplex ouvrent çà et là des perspectives en diagonale et font de la traversée de la maison une succession intéressante d'impressions spatiales très diverses, qualifiées par les architectes de « courts-circuits visuels ». La maison est construite en béton coulé sur place avec un coffrage perdu pour l'isolation thermique. Les murs intérieurs sont enduits de blanc, tous les sols et les éléments en bois sont en frêne. La façade se compose de panneaux de contreplaqué teintés de noir qui se chevauchent.

Das Haus in Stocksund ist als ein schmaler Block konzipiert, der quer auf dem zur Verfügung stehenden Baugrundstück steht und dieses in einen vorderen Bereich und einen Garten teilt. Das Haus ist daher fast ausschließlich frontal wahrnehmbar und wirkt wie eine bewohnbare Mauer. Im offenen Erdgeschoss sind Eingang und Treppe in einer Box zusammengefasst, die Individualräume im Obergeschoss werden über einen zentralen Gang erschlossen. Zweigeschossige Räume erlauben immer wieder diagonale Durchblicke und lassen den Weg durch das Gebäude zu einer interessanten Folge sehr unterschiedlicher Raumeindrücke werden, die von den Architekten als „visuelle Kurzschlüsse" bezeichnet werden. Die Konstruktion des Hauses besteht aus Ortbeton mit Wärmedämmung als verlorener Schalung. Die Innenwände sind weiß verputzt, alle Fußböden und Holzdetails sind aus Eschenholz. Die Fassade besteht aus einander überlappenden schwarz gebeizten Sperrholztafeln.

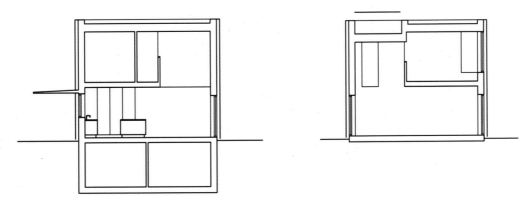

Cross-section · Section transversale · Querschnitt

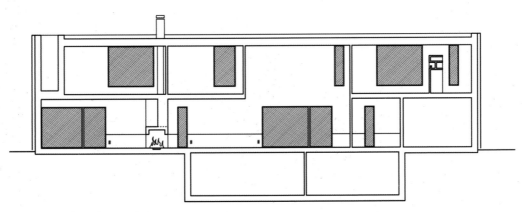

Longitudinal section · Section longitudinale · Längsschnitt

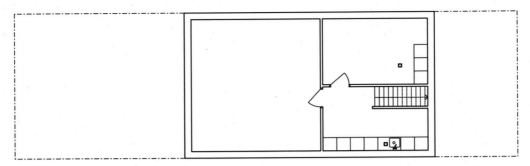

Basement · Sous-sol · Kellergeschoss

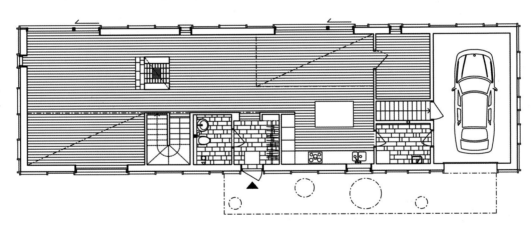

Ground floor · Rez-de-chaussée · Erdgeschoss

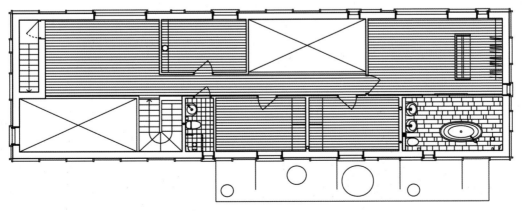

First floor · Premier étage · Erstes Obergeschoss

The building's lack of depth makes the interior rooms very bright. A fireplace open on both sides separates the living room from the dining room.

La faible profondeur du bâtiment fait paraître les pièces très claires et lumineuses. Une cheminée ouverte des deux côtés sépare l'espace salon de la salle à manger.

Durch die geringe Tiefe des Baukörpers wirken die Räume im Inneren sehr licht und hell. Ein nach beiden Seiten offener Kamin trennt den Wohn- vom Essbereich.

Interiors
Intérieurs
Innenansichten

Holiday House on the Rigi

Scheidegg, Switzerland, 2004
Andreas Fuhrimann Gabrielle Hächler Architects
Photos © Valentin Jeck

This detached house is set well away from neighbouring houses on the outskirts of town. It consists of a wooden structure which projects over a concrete storey. All three levels can be reached by two single-flight staircases positioned one above the other. The house is arranged around an open concrete fireplace at the widest point of the polygonal layout. The storey which houses the living room is in the middle of the house and has two levels, each with different ceiling heights. All the visible surfaces in the living room are wood-covered, just like the outside of the house. Large wooden sliding doors achieve close contact between the inside and the outside. The five-metre-wide panoramic window frames the breathtaking view of the Alps. The contrast between the grandeur of the mountain range and the homeliness of the low room is reflected inside, where coarse concrete is set off against delicately worked wood.

Cette maison individuelle est située à l'écart des maisons voisines, à l'entrée du village. Elle se compose d'un bloc en bois posé sur un niveau en béton au-dessus duquel elle forme un large surplomb. Les trois étages sont desservis par deux escaliers ouverts à une volée. À l'endroit le plus large de la structure polygonale se trouve une cheminée ouverte de béton autour de laquelle s'agence la maison. L'étage du séjour, au milieu, dispose de deux niveaux à hauteurs de plafond différentes. Toutes les surfaces visibles sont habillées de bois, de même que la façade. Des fenêtres coulissantes grand format en bois relient étroitement l'intérieur et l'extérieur. La fenêtre panoramique de cinq mètres de large encadre la vue extraordinaire sur les Alpes. Le contraste entre les montagnes majestueuses et la salle basse et douillette trouve un écho à l'intérieur, où s'opposent le béton grossier et le bois finement travaillé.

Das Einfamilienhaus liegt weit abgerückt von den Nachbarhäusern am Ortsrand. Es besteht aus einem hölzernen Volumen, das auf einem Betongeschoss aufgelegt ist und über dieses weit auskragt. Die insgesamt drei Ebenen werden von zwei übereinander liegenden einläufigen, offenen Treppen erschlossen. An der breitesten Stelle des polygonalen Grundrisses befindet sich ein offener Betonkamin, um den herum das Haus organisiert ist. Das mittig liegende Wohngeschoss verfügt über zwei Ebenen mit jeweils unterschiedlichen Deckenhöhen. Alle sichtbaren Flächen im Wohnbereich sind, wie auch die Fassade, mit Holz verkleidet. Großformatige hölzerne Schiebefenster stellen einen engen Kontakt zwischen Innen und Außen her. Das fünf Meter breite Panoramafenster umrahmt den atemberaubenden Blick auf die Alpen. Der Kontrast zwischen der Erhabenheit des Alpenmassivs und der Geborgenheit der niedrigen Wohnstube wird im Inneren durch den Gegensatz von grobem Beton und fein bearbeitetem Holz widergespiegelt.

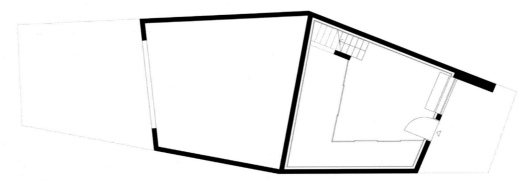

Basement · Sous-sol · Kellergeschoss

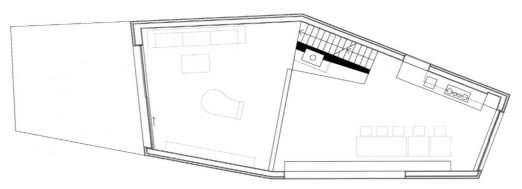

Ground floor · Rez-de-chaussée · Erdgeschoss

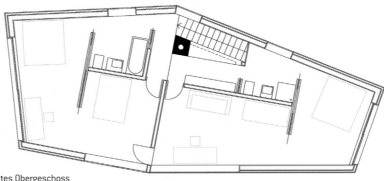

First floor · Premier étage · Erstes Obergeschoss

e bedrooms on the first floor are completely clad in wood and afford fantastic sweeping views of the Alps.
es chambres à coucher du premier étage sont entièrement lambrissées de bois et offrent une vue splendide sur les Alpes.
e Schlafräume im ersten Obergeschoss sind vollkommen mit Holz verkleidet und gewähren einen phantastischen Ausblick
uf das Alpenpanorama.

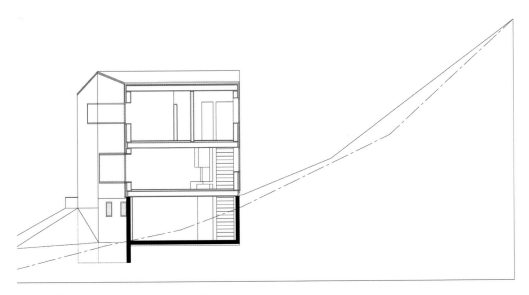

Cross-section · Section transversale · Querschnitt

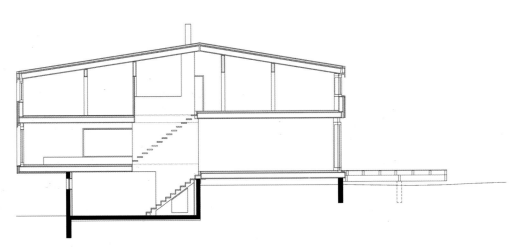

Longitudinal section · Section longitudinale · Längsschnitt

House at the Foot of the Uetliberg

Zurich, Switzerland, 2004
Andreas Fuhrimann Gabrielle Hächler Architects
Photos © Valentin Jeck

This apartment building lies at the foot of Uetli Mountain, on the outskirts of Zurich. The complex arrangement of the four different-sized apartments within the polygonal building provides them all with the same view over the city and the extensive plot of land. The cellar, the entrance steps and the apartment dividing walls are built from in-situ concrete that has been left in its natural raw state and forms the sculptural skeleton of the structure. The remaining walls and ceilings are crafted from prefabricated, insulated wooden elements. The coarse plywood walls and the more delicate three-layer board on the ceilings are left visible. The contrast between the coarse in-situ concrete and the industrially-manufactured wooden boards is a design principle here. This principle can also be seen in the custom-made colourful kitchens and the large, brightly-coloured vitrages in the bathrooms. The façade is clad in galvanised sheeting. The north side, facing the city, features large fixed glazing with no visible framework. Larchwood vents make reference to the wooden construction from the outside.

L'immeuble est situé au pied de l'Uetliberg, en périphérie de Zurich. L'imbrication complexe des quatre appartements de tailles différentes dans le volume polygonal permet à chacun de bénéficier d'une vue sur la ville et sur le vaste terrain environnant. Le matériau du sous-sol, des escaliers et des murs qui séparent les appartements est un béton coulé sur place à l'aspect rugueux. Il compose le squelette du bâtiment. Les autres murs et les plafonds sont en éléments de bois préfabriqués et isolés. Le grossier contreplaqué de caisserie des murs et le stratifié trois couches plus fin des plafonds ont été laissés apparents. Le contraste entre le béton coulé sur place et le bois de fabrication industrielle répond à un concept décoratif qu'on retrouve dans les cuisines colorées et les grands vitrages de couleurs des sanitaires. La façade est habillée de tôles galvanisées. Le côté nord, vers la ville, se distingue par de grandes baies vitrées sans cadre apparent. Des panneaux d'aération en mélèze rappellent la construction en bois.

Das Mehrfamilienhaus liegt am Fuß des Uetlibergs am Rande von Zürich. Durch die komplexe Verschachtelung der vier unterschiedlich großen Wohnungen innerhalb des polygonalen Volumens gewähren sie alle gleichermaßen die Aussicht auf die Stadt wie auch auf das weitläufige Grundstück. Das Kellergeschoss, die Erschließungstreppen und die Wohnungstrennwände sind in rau belassenem Ortbeton gebaut, der so das skulpturale Skelett des Baukörpers bildet. Die übrigen Wände und Decken sind aus vorfabrizierten, isolierten Holzelementen gefertigt. Das grobe Kistensperrholz der Wände und die feinere Dreischichtplatte der Decken sind sichtbar belassen. Der Kontrast zwischen dem groben Ortbeton und den industriell hergestellten Holzplatten wird zum Gestaltungsprinzip, das sich auch an den maßgefertigten farbigen Küchen und großflächigen bunten Glasverkleidungen in den Nasszellen erkennen lässt. Die Fassade besitzt eine Verkleidung aus verzinkten Blechen. Die zur Stadt gerichtete Nordseite ist durch großformatige Festverglasungen ohne sichtbaren Rahmen geprägt. Lüftungsklappen aus Lärchenholz verweisen von außen auf den Holzbau.

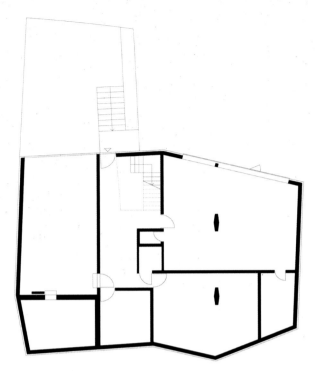

Ground floor · Rez-de-chaussée · Erdgeschoss

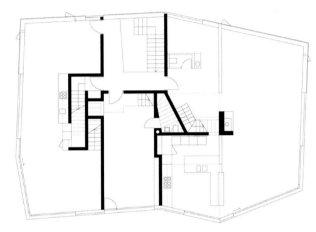

First floor · Premier étage · Erstes Obergeschoss

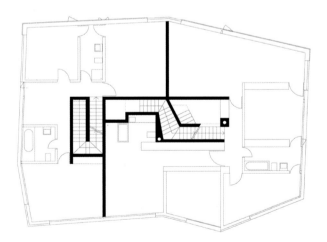

Second floor · Deuxième étage · Zweites Obergeschoss

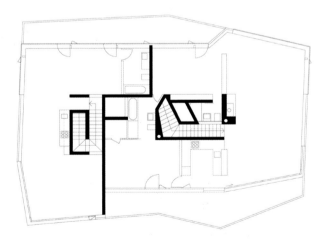

Penthouse · Appartement terrasse · Dachgeschoss

Inside, we can clearly recognise the design principle based on the contrast between concrete and wooden surfaces.
À l'intérieur, on retrouve sans peine le concept créatif basé sur le contraste entre les surfaces en béton et celles en bois.
In den Innenräumen ist deutlich das gestalterische Prinzip der Kontrastierung von Beton- und Holzflächen zu erkennen.

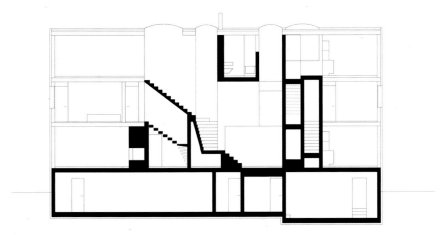

Longitudinal section · Section longitudinale · Längsschnitt

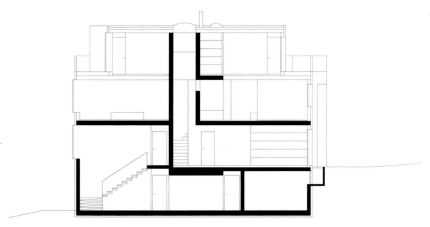

Cross-section · Section transversale · Querschnitt

Cape Schanck House

Victoria, Australia, 2006
Paul Morgan Architects
Photos © Peter Bennetts

This building, standing among sturdy tea trees, appears to be shying away from the strong winds blowing in from the sea. The architects took their inspiration from the bizarre shape of the tea tree and the gusty winds when designing the shape of the building shell. The living room is dominated by a water tank that "grows" organically from the ceiling. This tank fulfils several purposes: it collects rain water, cools room temperatures in summer and acts as a support, helping to bear the load of the roof. Even the characteristic wind aprons on the southern façade have multiple functions: they catch the wind in summer and thereby contribute to cooling the house, yet they also act as protection against the hot midday sun. The façade and inside walls are covered with treated plywood. Sculptural wooden elements, made from tropical merbau wood, feature at the entrance and on the terrace.

Entouré d'imposants théiers, ce bâtiment semble se ramasser sur lui-même pour esquiver les bourrasques qui soufflent de la mer. Les architectes se sont inspirés des étranges silhouettes des arbres et du vent en rafales pour l'enveloppe du bâtiment. L'espace habité est dominé par un réservoir d'eau qui se déploie organiquement à partir du plafond. Il réunit plusieurs fonctions : recueillir l'eau de pluie, l'utiliser pour refroidir l'air de la pièce en été et soutenir le toit. Les auvents caractéristiques de la façade sud ont eux aussi des fonctions multiples : ils aspirent le vent en été pour contribuer au rafraîchissement de la maison, qu'ils protègent aussi du chaud soleil de l'après-midi. Les façades et les cloisons sont recouvertes de contreplaqué enduit. Des éléments aux formes sculpturales en bois tropical de merbau mettent en valeur l'entrée et la terrasse.

Das inmitten von mächtigen Teebäumen liegende Gebäude scheint sich vor dem heftigen Wind wegzuducken, der vom Meer herüberweht. Die Architekten ließen sich von den bizarren Formen des Teebaums und dem böigen Wind zu der besonderen Form der Gebäudehülle inspirieren. Der Wohnraum wird von einem Wassertank dominiert, der sich organisch aus der Decke entwickelt. Dieser Tank vereint mehrere Funktionen in sich: Er fängt das Regenwasser auf, kühlt im Sommer damit die Raumluft und wirkt darüber hinaus als Stütze, die die Last des Daches mit trägt. Auch die charakteristischen Windschürzen an der Südfassade haben eine Mehrfachfunktion: in ihnen soll sich im Sommer der Wind fangen und somit zur Kühlung des Hauses beitragen, sie dienen aber auch dem Schutz vor der heißen Nachmittagssonne. Die Fassade und Innenwände sind mit beschichtetem Sperrholz verkleidet. Skulptural geformte Holzelemente aus tropischem Merbau akzentuieren den Eingang und die Terrasse.

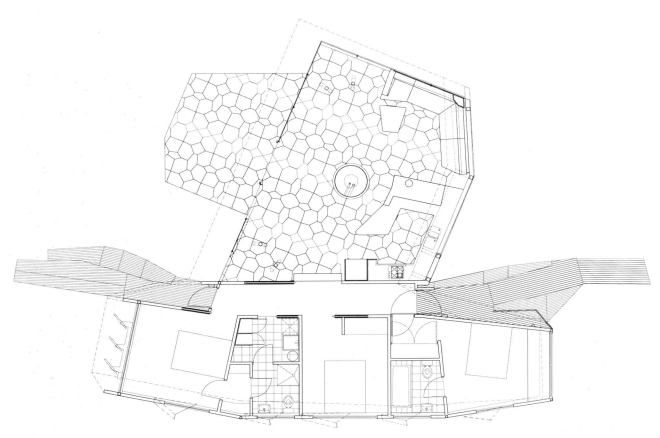

Plan · Plan · Grundriss

The bizarre shape of the tea tree inspired the architects in their unusual design of the house, which is shown to particular advantage at dusk.

Les formes étranges du théier ont fortement inspiré les architectes pour la forme inhabituelle de la maison, qui est particulièrement mise en valeur au crépuscule.

Die bizarr wirkenden Formen des Teebaums inspirierten die Architekten bei der außergewöhnlichen Ausführung des Hauses, die besonders in der Dämmerung zur Geltung kommt.

Pavi House

Bad Waltersdorf, Austria, 2002
Johannes Kaufmann Architektur
Photos © Paul Ott

This detached house, built on a narrow, sloping plot of land in a vineyard above the village, is minimalist yet spatially complex. The house is entered via the middle level, which protrudes far above the massive exposed foundation. The living room is on this level; the private quarters are on the upper floor and a guest room and wellness area with access to a swimming pool are in the basement. The very different levels are linked by a central indoor staircase, which is rather like a piece of furniture and divides the living area, tiled in dark, natural stone. The construction of solid wood and box-section elements is echoed inside the house in the bright, white fir wall panelling. The larchwood façade lies like a smooth curtain over the cubic structure. Only the protrusions and recesses of the large terraces, as well as the panoramic windows, break up the wooden cube, which resembles a fascinating abstract sculpture.

La maison individuelle, érigée sur une étroite bande de terrain en pente d'un vignoble dominant le village, est minimaliste, malgré l'organisation complexe de l'espace. On entre par le niveau médian qui s'avance loin au-dessus du socle massif. C'est là que se trouve le salon. La sphère privée se trouve à l'étage supérieur et le sous-sol se compose d'une chambre d'amis et d'un espace de détente donnant accès à la piscine. Les niveaux très différents sont reliés par un escalier intérieur central qui divise, tel un meuble, l'espace de séjour carrelé de pierres naturelles sombres. La construction de la maison, en bois massif et éléments-caissons, se reflète à l'intérieur sur le revêtement clair des murs en sapin blanc. La façade en lamelles de mélèze recouvre, tel un rideau, le bâtiment cubique. Seules les avancées et les découpures des grandes terrasses, ainsi que les fenêtres panoramiques, structurent le cube de bois qui ressemble à une fascinante sculpture abstraite.

Das Einfamilienhaus, auf einem schmalen, geneigten Grundstück eines Weinbergs über dem Ort erbaut, ist minimalistisch, aber räumlich komplex. Man betritt das Haus in der mittleren Ebene, die weit über den massiven Sockel auskragt. Hier befindet sich der Wohnbereich, im Obergeschoss liegen die Privaträume, und im Untergeschoss sind ein Gästezimmer und ein Wellnessbereich mit Zugang zum Swimming Pool untergebracht. Die sehr unterschiedlichen Ebenen werden durch eine zentrale Innentreppe miteinander verbunden, die im Wohnbereich wie ein Möbel den mit dunklem Naturstein gefliesten Raum aufteilt. Die Konstruktion des Hauses aus Massivholz- und Hohlkastenelementen bildet sich im Innern des Hauses durch die Verkleidung der Wände mit heller Weißtanne ab. Die Fassade aus Lärchenholzstäben legt sich wie ein glatter Vorhang um den kubischen Baukörper. Lediglich die Auskragungen und Einschnitte der großen Terrassen sowie die Flächen der Panoramafenster gliedern den Holzkubus, der so wie eine faszinierende abstrakte Skulptur wirkt.

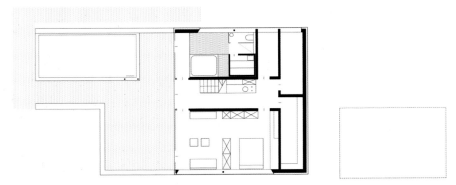

Basement · Sous-sol · Kellergeschoss

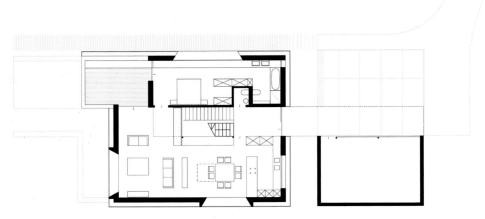

Ground floor · Rez-de-chaussée · Erdgeschoss

First floor · Premier étage · Erstes Obergeschoss

large windows on either side the comparatively small individual rooms make the latter appear considerably larger.

s grandes fenêtres sur deux côtés de chacune des pièces, par ailleurs relativement petites, les font paraître
aucoup plus grandes.

e großen Fenster, die die vergleichsweise kleinen Individualräume an jeweils zwei Seiten besitzen, lassen die Zimmer
sentlich größer erscheinen.

Amatepec House

Sierra Amatepec, Colonia Lomas de Chapultepec, Mexico City, Mexico, 2006
Manuel Cervantes Céspedes, CC Arquitectos
Photos © Luis Gordoa

This villa, situated outside Mexico City, has three floors. Topographical specifications meant that the building, which is home to a family as well as a modern-art collection, had to be a ferro-concrete construction. The house was designed as a generous suite of rooms providing a backdrop for art while offering privacy. The interior is therefore rather inward-looking and mostly indirectly lit. The very differently designed outside spaces are arranged to present a mirror image of the carefully-considered interior room sequence. These outside spaces are minimalist patios featuring sparse use of plants and intended to draw the eye to the interior. Flint and gravel make reference to the original rocky ground. The directed lighting and materials give the rooms a meditative calm, to which the continous pale parquet floor, in harmony with the largely white walls and ceilings, makes its own pronounced contribution.

La villa, à l'extérieur de Mexico, comprend trois niveaux au total. Pour des raisons topographiques, il a fallu construire le bâtiment, qui abrite une famille et une collection d'art moderne, en béton armé. La maison a été conçue comme une suite de vastes pièces qui mettent en scène les œuvres d'art qu'elles contiennent tout en garantissant l'intimité. Les pièces intérieures sont moins ouvertes sur l'extérieur et dotées d'un éclairage essentiellement indirect. Les espaces extérieurs, de conceptions très diverses, sont agencés de manière à former une image en miroir de la succession soigneusement pensée des pièces intérieures. Il s'agit de patios peu plantés et à l'aménagement minimaliste qui doivent avant tout attirer le regard vers l'intérieur. Le gravier rappelle le terrain rocheux d'origine. Du fait de l'éclairage et des matériaux utilisés, les pièces diffusent une atmosphère de calme propice à la méditation. Un parquet clair d'un seul tenant en accord avec les murs et les plafonds en grande partie blancs y contribue pour beaucoup.

Die außerhalb von Mexico City gelegene Villa verfügt über insgesamt drei Ebenen. Aufgrund der topographischen Vorgaben musste das Gebäude, das einer Familie ebenso Heimstatt ist wie einer Sammlung moderner Kunst, als Stahlbetonkonstruktion ausgeführt werden. Das Haus wurde als eine großzügige Raumfolge entworfen, die die Kunst inszeniert und zugleich Intimität gewährleistet. Die Innenräume sind daher eher introvertiert und meist indirekt beleuchtet. Die sehr unterschiedlich gestalteten Außenräume sind so angeordnet, dass sie zum Spiegelbild der mit Bedacht gewählten Abfolge der Innenräume werden. Sie sind minimalistisch gestaltete Patios mit sparsamer Bepflanzung, die vor allem nach Innen wirken sollen. Kies und Schotter verweisen auf das ursprüngliche, felsige Gelände. Aufgrund der Lichtführung und eingesetzten Materialien strahlen die Räume eine meditative Ruhe aus – ein kontinuierlicher, heller Parkettfußboden trägt im Einklang mit den im Wesentlichen in Weiß gehaltenen Wänden und Decken entscheidend dazu bei.

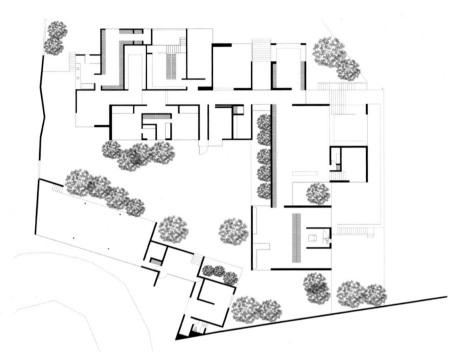

Site plan · Plan de situation · Lageplan

The interior lighting is mostly indirect, whether it is reflected by the white façade, penetrating the lateral light vents or
filtered through the plants on the patio.

L'éclairage des pièces intérieures est essentiellement indirect, qu'il soit reflété par le blanc de la façade, qu'il pénètre
par les interstices des côtés ou qu'il soit filtré par les plantes des patios.

Die Innenräume erhalten zumeist indirektes Licht, da es entweder durch das Weiß der Außenfassade reflektiert wird,
durch die seitlich angeordneten Lichtschlitze einfällt oder aber durch die Bepflanzung der Patios gefiltert wird.

Chalet in the Swiss Alps

Gstaad, Switzerland, 2000
Andreas Fuhrimann Gabrielle Hächler Architects
Photos © Fuhrimann Hächler

This mountain lodge, which had stood empty for more than 50 years, was remodelled for an art collector. From the outset, the architects' aim was to preserve the qualities and perfect proportions of this modest, functional building on wooden stilts. The traditional divisions of kitchen, stable and storage room can be seen in the chalet's floor plan. The newly-constructed kitchen and bathroom in the former storage room are built of solid stone from a local quarry. The building's ancient, almost black, log wall was preserved, and the roof was retiled with wood shingles. The details of the newly-fitted sliding windows echo local building traditions, but they allow the small room to be better used and furnished. The additional small sliding windows regulate airflow when lighting a fire.

Ce refuge de montagne, resté vide pendant plus de cinquante ans, a été transformé pour le compte d'un collectionneur d'art. Dès le début, les interventions des architectes ont visé à conserver les qualités et les proportions idéales de ce modeste bâtiment fonctionnel aux montants en bois. Le plan révèle le découpage traditionnel en cuisine, étable et cellier. Les nouvelles cuisine et salle de bains intégrées dans l'ancien cellier sont en pierres massives provenant d'une carrière des environs. Le mur ancestral du chalet, en tronçons de bois presque noirs, a été conservé et le toit couvert de nouveaux bardeaux. Les nouvelles fenêtres coulissantes rappellent par leurs détails les constructions traditionnelles locales, mais facilitent l'exploitation et l'ameublement des petites pièces. Les petites fenêtres supplémentaires aident à contrôler les courants d'air lors de l'allumage du feu.

Diese Berghütte, die mehr als fünfzig Jahre leer stand, wurde für einen Kunstsammler umgebaut. Die Eingriffe der Architekten zielten von Beginn an darauf ab, die Qualitäten des bescheidenen, auf Holzständern stehenden Zweckbaus mit seinen perfekten Proportionen zu bewahren. Der Grundriss der Hütte lässt die traditionelle Aufteilung in Küche, Stall und Vorratsraum erkennen. Die neu eingebaute Küche und das Bad in der ehemaligen Vorratskammer sind aus massivem Stein gefügt, der aus einem Steinbruch der Umgebung stammt. Die uralte, fast schwarze Holzblockwand des Hauses wurde bewahrt, das Dach wurde mit Holzschindeln neu eingedeckt. Die neu eingesetzten Schiebefenster verweisen in ihrer Detaillierung auf die örtliche Bautradition, erlauben aber eine bessere Ausnutzung und Möblierbarkeit der kleinen Räume. Die zusätzlichen kleinen Schiebefenster dienen zur Regulierung des Luftzugs beim Anfeuern des Kamins.

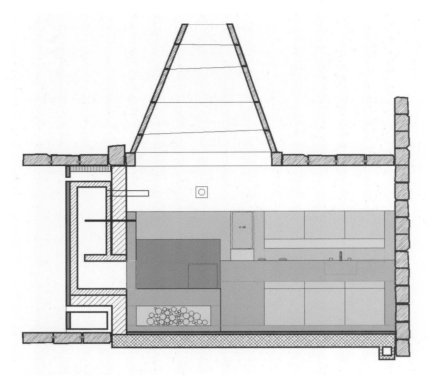

Section · Section · Schnitt

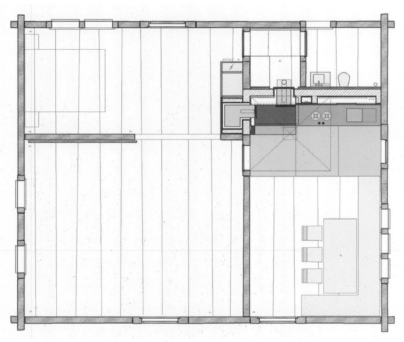

Plan · Plan · Grundriss

The carefully executed structural changes have not affected the original atmosphere of this centuries-old chalet.

Les modifications soigneusement réfléchies apportées au bâtiment n'ont en rien altéré le caractère rustique original du chalet vieux de plusieurs siècles.

Die mit Bedacht vorgenommenen baulichen Veränderungen haben die urwüchsige Atmosphäre der jahrhundertealten Hütte nicht beeinträchtigt.

Keel Cabin

White Face Reservoir, Minnesota, United States, 2003
Salmela Architect
Photos © Peter Bastianelli Kerze

This holiday home is located in the middle of the extensive forests of northern Minnesota. It is a real one-of-a-kind architectural treat. The architect compares the house – an expressive wooden construction that sits on concrete supports – to an animal that exudes cheerfulness and optimism despite adverse circumstances. A metal roof covers both the main house and a guesthouse – both exteriors are clad with dark, stained plywood boards. Wood also dominates the interior: the walls are made from birch plywood and the floors are laid with birchwood parquet. It was important not to exceed the tight budget throughout the building process. Thus, the varied, striking window formats originated from an initiative by the owner-builder, who, some time before the first design drafts, had the idea of buying unsold windows from manufacturers at discount prices. The architect made collage compositions of these windows, and they say a great deal about the individualistic spirit from which the house emerged.

Située au cœur des vastes forêts du Nord-Minnesota, cette maison de vacances constitue une pièce unique de par son originalité. Pour l'architecte, l'expressivité de la construction de bois sur ses piliers de béton rappelle un animal qui rayonne de gaieté et d'optimisme malgré des circonstances défavorables. Un toit métallique recouvre à la fois le bâtiment principal et la maison d'hôtes, tous deux habillés de panneaux de contreplaqué teintés en brun foncé. À l'intérieur aussi, le bois domine : les murs sont en contreplaqué de bouleau et les sols en parquet de bouleau. Pour tous les travaux, on a veillé à respecter le budget serré. Les formats surprenants des fenêtres sont dus à une initiative du maître d'ouvrage qui avait déjà commencé, longtemps avant les premiers plans de la maison, à débarrasser des fabricants de fenêtres de leurs invendus à des conditions spéciales. L'architecte en a fait des compositions qui en disent long sur l'état d'esprit individualiste qui a donné naissance à la maison.

Inmitten der weiten Wälder Nord-Minnesotas liegt dieses Ferienhaus, das in seiner Außergewöhnlichkeit ein echtes Unikat ist. Der Architekt vergleicht die auf Betonstützen gelagerte, expressiv wirkende Holzkonstruktion mit einem Tier, das trotz widriger Umstände Fröhlichkeit und Optimismus ausstrahlt. Ein Metalldach überspannt sowohl Haupthaus als auch Gästehaus, die beide mit dunkel gebeizten Sperrholzplatten verkleidet sind. Auch innen herrscht Holz vor – die Wände bestehen aus Birkensperrholz und die Fußböden sind mit Birkenholzparkett ausgelegt. Während des gesamten Bauprozesses galt es, die engen Kostenvorgaben nicht zu überschreiten. Die auffälligen, unterschiedlichen Fensterformate gehen auf eine Initiative des Bauherrn zurück, der schon geraume Zeit vor dem Entwurf des Gebäudes damit begonnen hatte, Fensterherstellern ihre nicht verkauften Fenster zu Sonderkonditionen abzunehmen. Der Architekt collagierte sie zu Kompositionen, die mehr über den individualistischen Geist aussagen, aus dem das Haus hervorgegangen ist, als es sonst vielleicht möglich gewesen wäre.

200

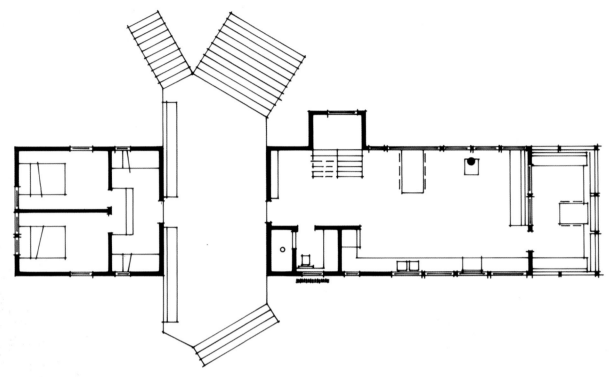

Ground floor · Rez-de-chaussée · Erdgeschoss

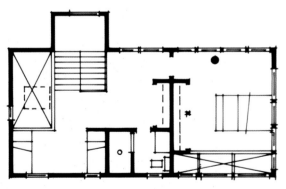

First floor · Premier étage · Erstes Obergeschoss

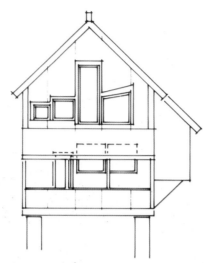

Side elevation · Élévation latérale · Seitenansicht

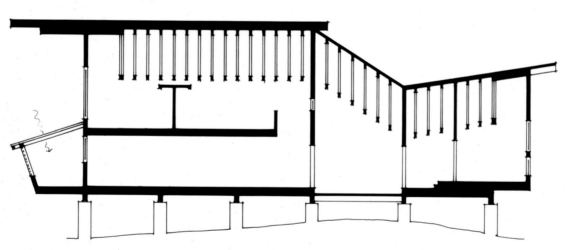

Longitudinal section · Section longitudinale · Längsschnitt

The unconventional appearance of the house, situated in the middle of the forest, gives it the air of an enchanted spot.

La maison au cœur de la forêt est une apparition si peu conventionnelle qu'elle en semble magique.

Das mitten im Wald stehende Haus wirkt durch seine vollkommen unkonventionelle Erscheinung wie ein verzauberter Ort.

5515 Penn

Pittsburgh, Pennsylvania, United States, 2007
Cruze Architects
Photos © Craig Thompson, Ed Massery, Liza Cruze

This former 1920s' warehouse, which has served as everything from a car dealership to a baker's and a dance studio, has been transformed by the architects into their own office. The ground floor now consists of the office, an architecture bookshop and a gallery. Upstairs there are three loft apartments. In their triple role as designers, principal builders and construction company, the architects found it particularly important to maintain control of the conversion from the planning stages to completion of the project in order to ensure an exceptional architectural quality. When the former dance studio was converted into a loft, the oak floorboards were preserved wherever possible. The sections of the dance floor which had to be removed because of the new room divisions were reused as panelling. The impressive wooden roof construction was left exposed so the space could expand upwards. In this way, and by limiting the number of materials used, this loft has a genuinely simple flair.

Cet ancien entrepôt des années 1920, qui a abrité successivement un concessionnaire automobile, une boulangerie et un studio de danse, a été transformé par les architectes qui en ont fait leur bureau. Le rez-de-chaussée comprend aujourd'hui le bureau, une librairie d'architecture et une galerie, tandis que l'étage abrite trois lofts. En assumant le triple rôle de concepteurs, maîtres d'ouvrage et exécutants, les architectes ont particulièrement tenu à garder la main sur l'ensemble des transformations, des premières esquisses aux dernières finitions, pour atteindre une qualité architecturale exceptionnelle. Lors de la transformation du studio de danse en loft, le parquet de chêne a été conservé pour l'essentiel. Les parties que la nouvelle disposition de l'espace a rendu nécessaire de retirer ont été réutilisées pour habiller les murs. L'imposante charpente en bois a été dégagée, ce qui a ouvert un nouvel espace vers le haut. Cette mesure, ainsi que le nombre réduit de matériaux utilisés, confèr au loft le charme sûr de l'authentique sobriété.

Das ehemalige Lagerhaus aus den 1920er Jahren, das im Laufe seiner Geschichte unter anderem einem Autohandel, einer Bäckerei und einem Tanzstudio Platz bot, wurde von den Architekten zu ihrem eigenen Büro umgebaut. Im Erdgeschoss befinden sich nun das Büro, eine Architekturbuchhandlung und eine Galerie, im Obergeschoss drei Loftwohnungen. In ihrer dreifachen Rolle als Entwerfer, Bauherren und ausführende Firma war es den Architekten vor allem wichtig, den Umbau von der Planung bis zur Fertigstellung in der Hand zu behalten, um so eine besondere Qualität zu gewährleisten. Beim Umbau des einstigen Tanzstudios in ein Loft wurde der Boden aus Eichenholz weitestgehend bewahrt. Die Teile des Tanzbodens, die aufgrund der neuen Raumaufteilung entfernt werden mussten, wurden als Wandverkleidung wieder verwendet. Die eindrucksvolle Dachkonstruktion aus Holz wurde freigelegt, wodurch der Raum eine Weitung nach oben erfuhr. Auf diese Weise – und durch die Beschränkung auf wenige Materialien – verströmt dieses Loft das Flair einer gediegenen Schlichtheit.

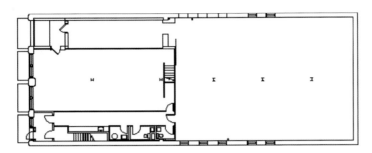

Ground floor · Rez-de-chaussée · Erdgeschoss

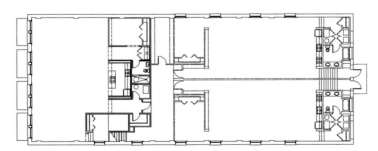

First floor · Premier étage · Erstes Obergeschoss

The historical façade facing the street is reserved in design: large display windows and an entrance area have replaced the former garage doors.

La façade historique sur la rue s'efface largement derrière le talent des créateurs. Les anciennes portes de garage ont fait place à de grandes vitrines et à l'entrée.

Die historische Fassade zur Straße nimmt sich gestalterisch stark zurück. An die Stelle der ehemaligen Garagentore sind große Schaufenster und der Eingangsbereich getreten.

Millhouse

Västra Karup, Skane, Sweden, 2000
Wingardh Arkitektkontor
Photos © Åke E:son Lindman

This refurbished mill, which is in Scania, southern Sweden, was intended by the architects to be a retreat from everyday life. The architects converted the ground floor into a large living room with an open-plan kitchen and a sauna. The open sleeping level below the roof is reached via a straight staircase. It is a tent-like, wonderfully simple space, which exudes great calm. The design of the living level, on the other hand, is very complex. A platform on the natural stone floor creates spatial hierarchy, while large surfaces of wood and exposed concrete accentuate the angles of the room. Continuous glass panels, some of which can be pushed to the side, provide close contact with the house's natural surroundings and the directly adjacent millpond. The open glass fireplace, which appears to be floating, is the focal point of the room. The house's impeccable detail, the quality of its execution and the successful harmony of wood and natural stone are impressive and further accentuated by the refined lighting.

Pour les architectes, il s'agissait de transformer cet ancien moulin de Scanie, dans le sud de la Suède, en un lieu de repos où se retirer du quotidien. Le rez-de-chaussée a été réservé à un grand salon, une cuisine ouverte et un sauna. Un escalier droit mène à l'espace ouvert qui tient lieu de chambre sous le toit, une pièce merveilleusement simple en forme de tente, qui dégage une impression de grand calme. Le niveau du séjour est en revanche agencé de manière extrêmement complexe. Un ensemble de dénivellations dans le sol de pierre naturelle établit une hiérarchisation des pièces dont de vastes surfaces de bois et de béton apparent soulignent les contours. Des vitres d'une pièce, coulissantes pour certaines, créent un contact étroit avec la nature environnante et l'étang, juste à côté. Au centre du salon, la cheminée ouverte en verre semble flotter. La maison frappe par un sens parfait du détail, une réalisation impeccable et l'harmonie réussie du bois et de la pierre, mis en valeur par un éclairage raffiné.

Die im südschwedischen Schonen gelegene Mühle sollte von den Architekten zu einem Rückzugsort vom Alltagsleben umgestaltet werden. Im Erdgeschoss sahen die Architekten einen großen Wohnbereich, eine offene Küche und eine Sauna vor. Über eine gerade Treppe erreicht man die offene Schlafebene unter dem Dach, ein zeltartiger, wunderbar einfacher Raum, der große Ruhe ausstrahlt. Die Wohnebene dagegen ist sehr komplex gestaltet. Ein Höhenversprung im Fußboden aus Naturstein schafft eine Hierarchie der Räume, große Holz- und Sichtbetonflächen akzentuieren die Raumkanten. Ungeteilte Glasflächen, die teilweise zur Seite geschoben werden können, stellen einen engen Kontakt zu der das Haus umgebenden Natur und dem direkt benachbarten Mühlteich her. Den Mittelpunkt des Wohnzimmers bildet der schwebend wirkende offene Kamin aus Glas. Das Haus beeindruckt durch seine perfekte Detaillierung, hochwertige Ausführung und die harmonische Kombination von Holz und Naturstein, die durch eine raffinierte Lichtführung zusätzlich unterstützt wird.

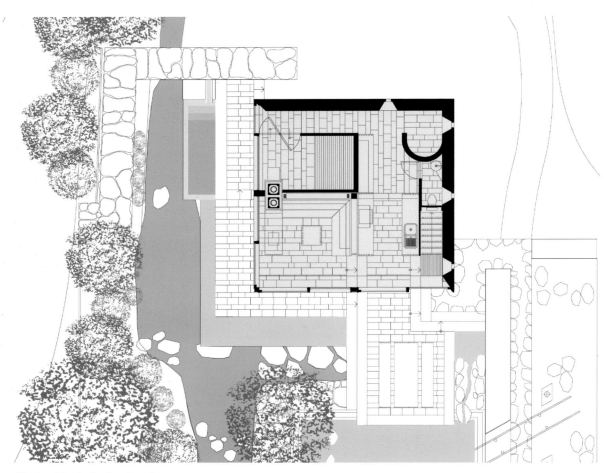

Site plan · Plan de situation · Lageplan

This house has a great deal of atmosphere despite its relatively small size thanks to the openness of the living room and its closeness to nature, the meditative calm of the sleeping level and the refined simplicity of the sauna area.

Avec l'ouverture du salon sur la nature, le calme invitant à la méditation qui émane de la chambre et la simplicité raffinée du sauna, la maison a beaucoup à offrir malgré une superficie relativement réduite.

Durch die Offenheit und den Naturbezug des Wohnraums, die meditative Ruhe, die die Schlafebene ausstrahlt, und einen gediegenen Saunabereich hat das Haus trotz relativ kleiner Grundfläche atmosphärisch viel zu bieten.

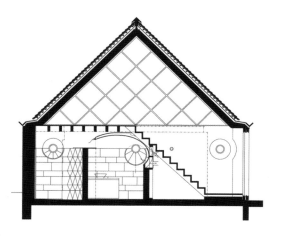

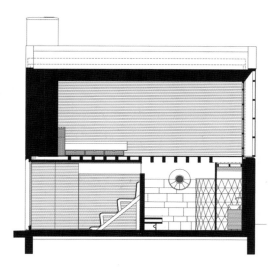

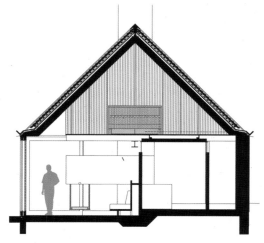

Sections · Sections · Schnitte

Mountain Shelter

Punta del Este, Uruguay
Martín Gomez Arquitectos
Photos © Daniel Mac Adden

This picturesque holiday home can be found in the shelter of a pine forest a few metres from the beach. The owner-builders are a young couple who spend their summer holidays here and want to use the house additionally for short stays. Owing to the limited budget, a simple wooden construction was designed from the existing two-building property. The two-storey, tower-like main house is linked by a large terrace to a single-storey house for guests. Pinewood is present throughout the property. Outside, the dark-painted house and the pine forest appear to merge into one. Inside, the use of whitewashed pinewood on the walls, ceilings and staircases creates a very homey atmosphere. In the summer months, the wooden terrace, which is partially covered by a pergola, becomes in effect the main living area.

Cette pittoresque maison de vacances est nichée à l'abri d'une forêt de pins, à seulement quelques mètres de la plage. Les maîtres d'ouvrage sont un jeune couple qui prévoit d'y passer les vacances d'été et de l'utiliser pour de courts séjours. En raison d'un budget limité, l'ensemble de deux bâtiments a été conçu comme une simple construction de bois. L'habitation principale à deux étages, en forme de tour, est reliée à la maison d'hôtes d'un étage par une vaste terrasse. Le bois de pin utilisé comme matériau de construction est omniprésent. À l'extérieur, la maison peinte de couleur sombre semble se fondre dans la forêt de pins avec laquelle elle ne forme plus qu'un. À l'intérieur, le pin lasuré blanc utilisé pour les murs, les plafonds et l'escalier crée une atmosphère très douillette. Pendant les mois d'été, la terrasse en bois partiellement recouverte d'une pergola devient le principal espace de vie de la maison.

In der Geborgenheit eines Kiefernwaldes, wenige Meter vom Strand entfernt, befindet sich dieses malerische Ferienhaus. Die Bauherren sind ein junges Paar, das hier den Sommerurlaub verbringen und das Haus ansonsten für kurze Aufenthalte nutzen will. Aufgrund des beschränkten Budgets wurde die aus zwei Gebäuden bestehende Anlage als einfache Holzkonstruktion konzipiert. Das zweigeschossige, turmartige Haupthaus ist durch eine große Terrasse mit einem eingeschossigen Gästehaus verbunden. Der Baustoff Kiefernholz ist überall in der Anlage präsent. Im Außenbereich scheint das dunkel gestrichene Haus mit dem Kiefernwald zu einer Einheit zu verschmelzen. Innen sorgt die Verwendung von weiß lasiertem Kiefernholz an Wänden, Decken und an der Treppe für eine sehr wohnliche Atmosphäre. In den Sommermonaten ist die hölzerne Terrasse, die teilweise mit einer Pergola überdeckt ist, der eigentliche Wohnraum des Hauses.

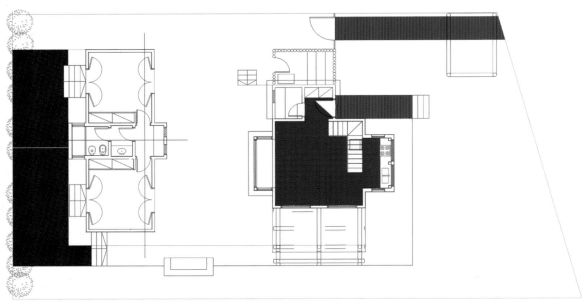

Plan · Plan · Grundriss

Surrounding the small house on all sides, the pine forest makes itself felt in every room and brings a feeling of security.

Entourant la petite maison de tous côtés, la forêt de pins visible depuis toutes les pièces procure un sentiment de sécurité confortable aux habitants.

Der Kiefernwald, der das kleine Haus von allen Seiten umschließt und damit in jedem Raum erfahrbar ist, lässt bei seinen Bewohnern ein Gefühl der Geborgenheit entstehen.

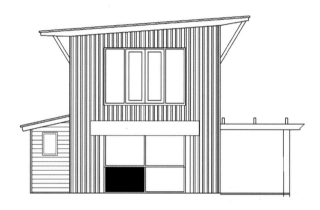

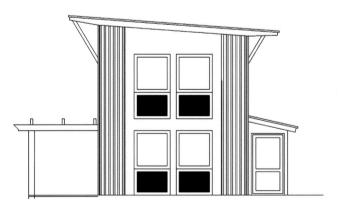

Elevations · Élévations · Aufrisse

Contemporary Cabin

Chiloé, Chile, 2003
Alberto Moletto, Ignacio Pardo
Photos © Fernando Gómez Morales

This holiday home on Chiloé Island in southern Chile, which at first glance appears simple and modest, turns out to have an exciting spatial structure. Owing to its remote location on a hillside, the house is reached via a boardwalk, and the entrance is on the first floor. The living room is a floor below, but it uses the entire height of the two-storey building. A large bank of windows opens up sweeping views over the water. The chief attraction of the house is the roof terrace, which is reached via an outside stairway and is enclosed only by a railing made from delicate, horizontally stretched wires. Wood is the main material used in the house. All the façades are covered with wooden shingles that have weathered to silver-grey. Inside, the floors, walls, ceilings and all the furniture are made of wood. All over the house, window openings of various shapes and sizes allow a close relationship to the surrounding nature.

À première vue simple et modeste, cette maison de vacances située sur l'île Chiloé, dans le sud du Chili, dévoile une structure fascinante dès qu'on y pénètre. En raison de sa situation isolée à flanc de coteau, elle est accessible par une passerelle en bois, l'entrée se trouvant au premier étage. La salle de séjour proprement dite est située un étage plus bas, mais occupe toute la hauteur du bâtiment à deux niveaux. Une grande baie vitrée ouvre une large vue sur la mer. Le toit en terrasse, la cerise sur le gâteau, est desservi par un escalier extérieur et uniquement entouré d'une balustrade de minces fils métalliques tendus horizontalement. Le matériau dominant est le bois. Toutes les façades sont couvertes de bardeaux auxquels les intempéries donnent une teinte gris argenté. À l'intérieur, les sols, murs, plafonds et tous les meubles sont en bois. Partout, des embrasures de fenêtres aux proportions diverses permettent un rapport étroit avec la nature qui entoure la maison.

Das auf den ersten Blick einfach und bescheiden erscheinende Ferienhaus, das auf der Insel Chiloé im südlichen Chile gelegen ist, erweist sich beim Betreten als spannendes räumliches Gefüge. Aufgrund der abgeschiedenen Lage an einem Hang kann das Haus nur über einen Holzsteg erreicht werden, der Eingang befindet sich in der ersten Etage. Der eigentliche Wohnraum liegt eine Etage tiefer, nutzt aber die ganze Höhe des zweigeschossigen Gebäudes. Eine große Fensterfront eröffnet einen weiten Blick auf das Wasser. Der Clou des Hauses ist die Dachterrasse, die über eine Außentreppe erschlossen wird und lediglich mit einem Geländer aus feinen, horizontal gespannten Drähten eingefasst ist. Holz ist das bestimmende Material des Hauses. Alle Fassaden sind mit Holzschindeln verkleidet, die sich in der Witterung silbergrau verfärben. Innen sind Fußböden, Wände, Decken und alle Möbel aus Holz gefertigt. Individuell proportionierte Fensteröffnungen stellen überall im Haus einen engen Bezug zu der das Haus umgebenden Natur her.

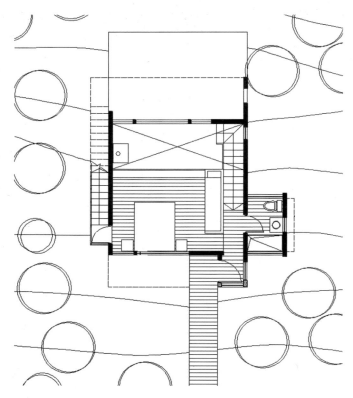

Ground floor · Rez-de-chaussée · Erdgeschoss

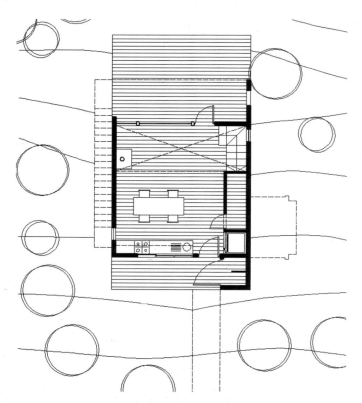

First floor · Premier étage · Erstes Obergeschoss

The entrance to the house is on the upper floor, which houses the bedrooms and is open to the living room below.

L'entrée de la maison est située à l'étage supérieur, où se trouve également la chambre à coucher ouverte sur le salon à l'étage inférieur.

Der Eingang des Hauses befindet sich in der oberen Etage, in der die Schlafebene liegt, die zum Wohnraum darunter offen ist.

Summerhouse

Tjuvkil, Sweden, 2003
Wingardh Arkitektkontor
Fotos © Ulf Celander

The holiday home located north of Gothenburg lies in the middle of a spectacular coastal landscape. This property mixes great elegance with an impressively simple structure. As the plot of land can only be reached by water, the architects decided on a wooden construction. The typical shape of the house is derived from traditional local buildings. The durable wooden façade made from untreated Canadian cedar wood requires almost no maintenance. In the middle of the strictly symmetrical house, the living room extends to the roof and is flanked to the left and right by an open-plan kitchen, dining room and bedroom. Two symmetrically-aligned staircases each provide access to a bedroom directly beneath the roof. Almost all the wooden elements inside the house are painted white. The impressive, huge panoramic windows which look out to sea can be partially slid to one side. In addition, a long series of skylights directly under the ridge ensures that a profusion of natural light enters the house.

Cette maison d'été, située au nord de Göteborg et au cœur d'un imposant paysage côtier, se caractérise par une grande élégance et une structure qui séduit par sa simplicité. Le terrain étant uniquement accessible en bateau, les architectes ont donc opté pour une construction en bois. La forme typique de la maison est inspirée des bâtiments traditionnels de la région. La solide façade en cèdre du Canada non traité n'exige presque aucun entretien. Au milieu de l'ensemble parfaitement symétrique, le salon, qui occupe l'espace jusqu'au toit, est flanqué à gauche et à droite d'une cuisine ouverte, d'une salle à manger et d'une chambre à coucher. Deux escaliers symétriques rejoignent chacun une chambre située juste sous le toit. À l'intérieur, presque tous les éléments en bois sont laqués en blanc. Les immenses fenêtres panoramiques donnant sur la mer, coulissantes pour certaines, sont particulièrement impressionnantes. Une longue rangée de fenêtres percées dans le toit, juste sous le faîte, laisse entrer la lumière à profusion.

Das Sommerhaus, nördlich von Göteborg inmitten einer eindrucksvollen Küstenlandschaft gelegen, ist von einer großen Eleganz und von einer bestechend einfachen Struktur geprägt. Da das Grundstück lediglich vom Wasser aus zugänglich ist, entschieden sich die Architekten für eine Holzkonstruktion. Die archetypisch wirkende Form des Hauses ist von den traditionellen Gebäuden der Gegend abgeleitet. Die dauerhafte Holzfassade aus unbehandeltem kanadischem Zedernholz erfordert fast keine Instandhaltungsarbeiten. Inmitten des streng symmetrisch gegliederten Hauses liegt der bis unter das Dach reichende Wohnraum, der links und rechts durch eine offene Küche, den Essraum und das Schlafzimmer flankiert wird. Zwei parallele Treppen erschließen jeweils eine direkt unter dem Dach liegende Schlafebene. Fast alle Holzbauteile im Inneren sind weiß lackiert. Eindrucksvoll sind die riesigen Panoramafenster zum Meer hin, die sich teilweise zur Seite schieben und öffnen lassen. Über eine lange Reihe von direkt unter dem First gelegenen Dachfenstern fällt zusätzlich reichlich Licht in das Haus.

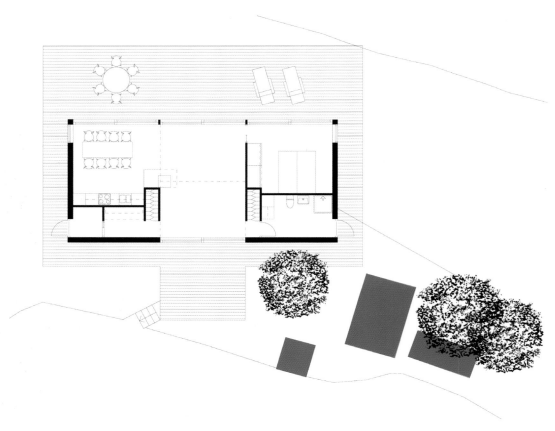

Plan · Plan · Grundriss

A large wooden terrace surrounds the building on all four sides. A flight of steps leads down to the landing stage.

Une grande terrasse en bois entoure la maison des quatre côtés. Un escalier en descend vers le ponton.

Eine große Holzterrasse umgibt das Gebäude an allen vier Seiten. Eine Treppe führt hinunter zum Bootssteg.